# THE SNIPER'S HANDBOOK

# THE SNIPER'S HANDBOOK

## THE 3 LAWS OF BASKETBALL SHOOTING POWER & ACCURACY

# Mark F. Johnston

Published by

TreasureLifeMedia.Com

# Sniper's Handbook: The 3 Laws of Basketball Shooting Power & Accuracy

Printed in the United States of America. First Edition, March 2020

ISBN: 978-0-9663917-2-5

Categories: Sports, Self-Improvement, Basketball, Fitness

Disclaimer: I am not a certified trainer or medical professional, and this book is not intended to be medical advice. All readers and owners of this book agree to hold me totally harmless if you get injured. You do these exercises at your own risk and accept full responsibility for your own health and wellness. Always check with your doctor before engaging in an exercise program. Also, the shooting system documented in this book is not based on one player but rather an amalgamation of players who share similar shooting techniques. This is a fully independent educational work published by TreasureLifeMedia.com to help people learn how to shoot more powerfully and accurately. All imagery and artwork are original and any resemblance to any person living or dead is purely coincidental.

## Dedication

From one hoopster to another, this book is dedicated to YOU. To your love of the game, to your decision and commitment to improve, to your passion, to your dreams of record-breaking performances in hoops and life. No matter your age, from 1 to 110, may you never stop striving to shatter every glass ceiling and break every record.

## 🙏 Thank You 🙏

God Almighty and His Son, without whom this work would not be possible. To my best friend and wife Rebecca; our beloved children, Deric, Leena; my mom Gloria and dad Fred (RIP). To all my military brothers and sisters and LEO whose protection of my freedoms allow me to play hoops in the first place. To all the innovators who saw further. To everyone who has encouraged and challenged me to go above and beyond my imagined limits and abilities. It is from a foundation of humble gratitude and motivation to "pay it forward" and share all the gifts the Lord has shared with me that I present this work.

*"You are never too old to set another goal, or to dream a new dream." – C.S. Lewis*

*"The people who are crazy enough to think they can change the world are the ones who do." — Steve Jobs*

*#MoonShot*

# Lethal Contents

*JUSTIFY LINES!*

# Welcome to the Lethal Revolution

*SPACES BETWEEN PARAGRAPHS*

*Lethal (adj): gravely dangerous, damaging, or destructive: DEVASTATING. Very potent or effective. I.e., "A lethal attack on his reputation."*

Dear fellow hoopster (don't sleep on this intro.) Every word of this book has been carefully thought out and will help you become a LETHAL (powerful, accurate, and efficient) basketball shooter—IF your mind and heart are open to humbly learning, patiently understanding, and devotedly applying the knowledge and wisdom in these pages. I guarantee it. If it doesn't improve your power and accuracy at all, we'll refund you the price of the book minus shipping charges.

Hi, I'm Mark the Hoopster (formerly known as Frank Gamble—more on that in a minute), a systems and process engineer, shot reformer, author, and lifelong hoopster. THANK YOU for buying this book. I pray this work is a blessing for you in more ways than one.

In this brief but important introduction, I'll share the "Frank Gamble" revelations that motivated me to write this book (and why the knowledge I share in it applies to much more than shooting the basketball and winning games). I'll also provide an overview of the "3 Laws of

Shooting Lethality" and a few words about the book format.

# The Frank Gamble Revelations

> *"Sometimes if you want to see a change for the better, you have to take things into your own hands." —* Clint Eastwood

Several years ago, when I made a decision and commitment to *fix* my streaky jump shot, I turned to YouTube and many other sources for shot "hacks." I found hundreds of thousands of shooting coaches, trainers, players, and gurus of all sorts. I dove right into all the online resources and started learning, experimenting, and investing a lot of practice hours on the court.

Initially, my shot improved a little, and I was feeling good about it. But then something strange happened: the more I tried to "fix" my jump shot with new hacks, the streakier and more unpredictable it became. I finally had to take a break from all the shot doctors and reset because my field goal percentage had actually *decreased!*

*Coach's note:* I measured my field goal percentage by tracking how many 3-pointers I could make in 3 minutes (getting my own rebounds). I call this the "33" drill. I highly recommend testing yourself for three "33" rounds and writing down your average. It will be a good way to track your improvement.

Determined to succeed, I kept practicing, video recording my shot, and studying other great shooters. Then one day, something huge occurred to me: every time I shot the ball, my body was in a slightly different form and motion. That is, sometimes I shot with a straight torso, other times I shot with a tilted torso; sometimes I shot with a great follow-though, other times I didn't. I was totally inconsistent and totally unpredictable.

That was when my engineering experience kicked in and I realized I had never developed a step-by-step, repeatable method or "system" for shooting the ball. My shot was basically a patchwork of instincts and self-taught random hacks and that's why it had never improved greatly. I playfully referred to this realization as my "Frankenstein Revelation" because I had come to see my shot was more like a wacky science experiment gone wrong than a finely-tuned shooting machine.

Question to ponder: Is your shot a Frankenstein patchwork of self-taught hacks or a well-designed, reliable shooting system?

Within days of my Frankenstein Revelation, I realized why I was not a confident shooter and why shooting the basketball always felt like I was rolling dice: I never knew what the ball was going to do after it left my hands! No wonder I always got nervous before playing! My shot was based on luck, not technically-sound knowledge and the confidence that comes from knowledge. I light-heartedly referred to this as my "Gambler Revelation" because I had come to see I wasn't a Hoops Sniper but more like a Hoops Gambler!

Another question to ponder: Are you a Hoops Sniper or a Hoops Gambler?

Now you know: Frankenstein + Gambler = Frank Gamble. Remember this name because as you progress in knowledge and understanding you'll start realizing you and/or other players you know are also Frank Gambles rather than well-designed shooting machines. Hey, if nothing else, it's a fun conversation starter. Yes, we are going to get highly creative in this book. As Einstein said, "Creativity is intelligence having fun." And I am all about having fun. #FrankGamble.

My Frank Gamble revelations were major *breakthroughs* and turning points because they helped me finally understand why I had been a streaky shooter and why I had only made sluggish shooting improvement. My problem? I had been following my instincts and other people's fragmented advice when I should have been starting over and building a *new shooting system* from the ground up because my inconsistent shot was not producing the results I wanted. CHANGE was needed—not just incremental change, but reformative change.

I finally acknowledged that if I was going to improve a lot, I would need to do the same thing I did to learn how to engineer software, compose music, and many other things: toss out everything I knew about shooting and become a <u>student</u> of great shooters and the laws that govern shooting. Which laws? The laws of physics (the science of motion) and ballistics (the science of projectile motion).

# Lethal Revolution Launch

*"The secret to change is to focus all of your energy not on fighting the old, but on building the <u>new</u>."* — *Socrates*

Upon embarking on my new journey to *shooting truth*, I unsubscribed from all the "shot doctor" channels and got to work analyzing all the great shooters to understand how their shooting methods correlated to

13

scientific laws of physics, ballistics, kinetic energy, et al. My goal was to find a step-by-step method for shooting the ball in the most powerful, accurate, and efficient way possible.

After many hours of research, analysis, testing, talking to other players, and experimentation with different methods, I finally identified which shooting forms and motions offered the highest degree of power and accuracy. I called it the "Lethal Shot" because within a month or so of practicing it, I witnessed it had deadly (as in highly effective) consequences on the court.

Blown away by my rapid improvement, I was moved to pay it forward and share the Lethal shooting method with other players—not as a hack to "fix" their shots, but as a *new way* to shoot the ball. At first, I made videos, but then I realized for people to understand the Lethal shot, they would need more than demos. That's when I decided to engineer a step-by-step Blueprint to help people understand how each form and motion of the Lethal shot works together as a whole.

Once I completed the Blueprint, I assumed the perspective of a new student and got to work practicing and putting the step-by-step instruction to the test. I spent many hours in the gym working out the kinks, journaling my progress, and training other shooters. I was surprised to find the more people I explained it to and trained, the more I understood it myself and improved! FYI: Teaching a subject to others is the most effective way of learning.

When I was satisfied the Blueprint was on point, I consolidated my journal notes and formulated what I call the "First Law of Shooting Lethality: Right Form & Motion (Physics)." But just as I was about to start writing this book, a few surprising things happened that made me realize I was still missing a crucial piece of the puzzle.

First, strangely, the more I practiced the shot, especially in front of other players, the less reliable it became. Unable to shoot out of my slump, I started video recording my shot again to figure out what was happening. Lo and behold, I was shocked to find I had reverted to old shooting habits. It was shocking because *in my mind* I was *certain* I had been shooting correctly. I recalibrated my shot form and motion and soon was improving again.

Second, when I told people about the Lethal shot method, most were resistant to the idea and said they were "set" in their ways and didn't *believe* developing a new shot method would help them. I understood where they were coming from—especially since I felt the same way for a long time. I found myself coaching them more about overcoming their limiting beliefs than shooting the Lethal way.

*"Whether you think you can or*
*you can't—you're right!" — Henry*
*Ford*

After pondering those two things for a while, I
realized in both cases that a *limited or blocked state of
mind* was preventing me and others from improving. In
my case, my mind had tricked me into thinking I was
shooting the right way when I wasn't; in the case of
people who resisted change, their minds had tricked
them into thinking they couldn't get any better. Both of
us had *limiting beliefs* that prevented us from
progressing. It was then I realized the Sniper's
Handbook needed a second law regarding the
importance of having a "right state mind state."

What kind of "right" mind state? A limitless (or
"breakthrough") mind state as opposed to a limited or
"breakdown" mind state. A "breakthrough" mind state
refers to an open, free mind with the unlimited belief
that *anything is possible* rather than the limited belief
that only certain things are possible.

That was the day the "Second Law of Lethality:
"Right Mind State" came to be. After adding the third
Law, "The 12 NeXt Factors" (a collection of Lethal
upgrades that will improve your shot even more), I
grouped all three laws into one body of knowledge and
called it "BALListic Shot Technology." For reference,
when you apply technical knowledge to a practical use,

it's called a technology. The Sniper's Handbook was finally ready to write.

Next, I will provide a quick overview of the 3 Laws of Shooting Lethality, then add a few closing remarks about the book.

# 3 Laws of Shooting Lethality

> *"If you believe in science, like I do, you believe that there are certain laws that [must be] obeyed."*
> — Stephen Hawking

To organize the Ballistic Shot Technology and make it simple as possible, I consolidated all the knowledge and wisdom I have gathered into three laws that I believe must be obeyed to achieve maximum shooting Lethality. Each law has one purpose and one purpose only: to increase your shooting power, accuracy, and efficiency. Law #1 is physics-based and generates physical power; Law #2 is mindfully and spiritually-based and generates mind power; Law #3 is a set of 12 upgrades that will enrich and strengthen the first two laws and create even more power.

Also, the 3 Laws of Shooting Lethality correlate to the three sections of this book and they all work together to form full, mature shooting Lethality. Each law also represents a Sniper maturity level similar to purple, brown, and black belts in martial arts. #SniperLethalityLevels.

Next is a quick overview of the 3 Laws and Sniper Maturity Levels.

## LAW 1: Right Form & Motion (Physics)

Right Form & Motion (Physics) refers to the most optimal body forms and motions illustrated in the Lethal Blueprint that <u>your mind and body must harmoniously conform to</u> in order to generate maximum ballistic power to shoot the ball as accurately and efficiently as possible. I will be covering all forms and motions in detail in Section 1 of this book. This is Level 1 Sniper Lethality.

Here is a quick introduction of the Lethal Blueprint containing all the right forms and motions that Law #1 is based on.

### The Lethal Shot™ Blueprint

The Lethal Shot Blueprint contains the right body forms and motions your shooting machine must learn and master to be a Lethal Sniper. It is the culmination of deep research, analysis, and testing, and I will fully explain it in Section 1. The reason I'm sharing it in the introduction is so you can start visualizing it as soon as possible. Please take a moment to print the print-friendly version at the back of this book and use it as a bookmark so you always have it nearby for reference.

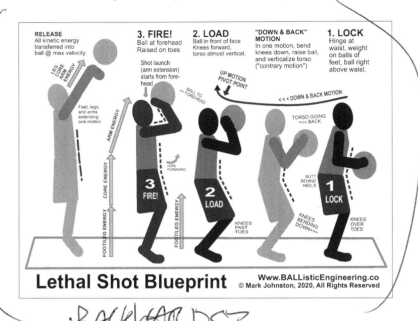

**Lethal Shot Blueprint**

Www.BALListicEngineering.co © Mark Johnston, 2020, All Rights Reserved

*BACKWARDS?*

Just a few brief comments about the Blueprint. Looking at the Blueprint from right to left, you'll see it captures the main forms and motions the body must execute from start to finish. Why does it go right to left? Because unlike most other jump shot methods, the Lethal shot does not start with a forward or upward body motion; it starts with a "down and back" motion and smoothly transitions to an "up" motion. To be sure, it's technically a two-motion shot that must be fused into one motion (which is easily one of—if not *the*—hardest part of mastering it). #MotionFusion

*Wait, what?*

If you're already scratching your head, don't worry; the Lethal way of shooting requires more than just a little explanation to understand (which is why I published a book rather than a YouTube video). For now, just look over the Blueprint, soak it in, and rest assured I will be explaining it thoroughly.

### LAW 2: Right Mind State

This refers to the necessity of having what I call an unlimited "breakthrough mind state," which is a *new way of limitless FREE thinking* needed to *create, enjoy, and truly excel* at basketball (or any creative pursuit). I'm not referring to how you think about shooting; I'm referring to how you *think*, period. In this section of the book I explain how I learned to have a limitless breakthrough mind state and how you can too. Understanding and applying these principles leads to Level 2 Sniper Lethality. #BreakthroughMindState #IAmUnlimited

### LAW 3: The 12 NeXt Factors™

The 12 NeXt Factors are a potent set of powerful *upgrades* in the realms of physics, mind and spiritual power, motive and purpose, self-discipline, dietary management, and more. You can go a long way with Laws 1 and 2, but with the 12 NeXt Factors you will ruthlessly shatter every glass ceiling you encounter. This is full Level 3 Sniper Lethality. #NeXtFactors

In summary, the 3 Laws of Shooting Lethality and 12 NeXt Factors contain everything you need to know to become a deadly Sniper. Those who are patient and take the time to understand the knowledge will be greatly positioned to obey them successfully on the court and achieve maximum victory. Never forget this: Knowledge is power and will get you far, but *understanding* is exponential power that will get you exponentially farther.

## About the Book

*"It is not that I'm so smart. I just stay with the questions much longer than other people." – Einstein*

I know what some people might be thinking: Who does this dude think he is to come out of "left field" and make such bold claims about shooting? I understand your skepticism. The idea that some Joe-Blow-college-dropout-street-baller with a systems engineering and change leadership background has blueprinted the most effective shot design in the known world and can teach it to anyone in their living room is, at a minimum, radical. I get it. If I were you several years ago, I would think I was crazy too.

But my claims aren't as crazy as they might seem. Why? Because the Lethal Blueprint is not some wild idea I pulled out of a hat. It's based on real world results and, more importantly, scientific laws. Moreover, it's not my idea. It's the idea of many great shooters who use this form and variations of it and great scientists that came before me. As the previous quote by Newton said, "If I am seeing further it's only because I am drawing from knowledge that existed before I came along." I'm just the guy who put all the knowledge together.

To be clear, I'm advancing a *new jump shot design.* I say it's "new" because it is not a common way to shoot. For you to understand it, I must take it apart and identify each form and motion of the shot with the hope that you will copy it, build on it, and maybe even improve it. This is a widely accepted scientific method, and I know it works because I've successfully used it throughout my career.

I should note: I am not suggesting you need to shoot EXACTLY like the Blueprint; but the closer you get to it, the more powerful and accurate you will be.

This book is for anyone of any age seeking a great physical and mental challenge. Little tikes to senior citizens, come one come all. My goal is to share knowledge and wisdom, challenge you, and hopefully light a little fire of inspiration in you. As for understanding, you will need to work that out through your own reasoning, visualization, and meditation. I can teach it to you, but to understand it, you will have to think about it... a lot.

> *"Isaac Newton was asked how he discovered the law of gravity. He replied, "By thinking about it all the time."* — *Isaac Newton*

This book is written for those whose minds and hearts are open to futuristic and new possibilities. The fertile soil for growth. The innovators. The dreamers. The record breakers. It's not only a book of laws and upgrades that can and will take your shot (and mind!) to a completely new level, but it's a motivational and inspirational *journal* of how I came to learn the secrets through relentless research, trial and error, testing, and unwavering commitment to breakthrough victory.

If you humbly learn and faithfully apply this wisdom, I am certain you too will have a breakthrough victory *and* be spared untold pain, time, money, and frustration—all of which will enable you to enjoy the game much more. #Victory

My hope is that this book challenges people to seek knowledge, learn, understand how things work, grow, enjoy playing, and use hoops to connect and share your gifts with others out of love and gratitude. The "Breakthrough" mind state I'm advancing in this book is not about breaking official record books; it's about breaking barriers of all kinds and realizing your full potential in many ways.

Also, I did not blueprint the Lethal jump shot and publish it to suggest that people should be obsessed with perfecting their jump shot and winning trophies. First, you can never be mechanically perfect, so the pursuit of perfection is futile. Second, trophies don't bring lasting joy. Third, I believe life is about finding and embracing your purpose, developing and sharing your gifts, and running this race with faith and endurance to be a blessing for God and others.

To reiterate, when I say "victory," I'm not necessarily referring to winning. I'm also not referring to being an aloof ball hog. The good life is love and teamwork. I'm talking about something much more profound than merely winning games. I've already hinted at it, but I will spell it out in the pages ahead.

Granted, if you're OK with staying just as you are, never evolving, and never improving beyond status quo—in other words, if you are content to be a 35% shooter at best—then this book isn't for you. You can become a 35%-er by watching YouTube videos and following conventional basketball wisdom. But if you are fully committed and devoted and dream of breaking records and soaring to new heights that people say you could *never* soar to—then this book IS for you, and I'm confident you are going to get exponentially more out of it than you paid.

How sure am I of this? Here's my guarantee: if you apply the wisdom in this book, and you don't make ANY shooting progress in 45 days, I will refund your purchase price for this book (minus shipping and handling). Done deal.

My journey to jump shot truth (power, accuracy, and efficiency) started with a decision and commitment. So, before you read another word, make a decision and commitment to improve your jump shot. Print the next page, tear off a section, write your commitment ("I have made the decision to improve my jump shot, and I am committed to being victorious!"), and then put it somewhere you will see it every day. Then take a pic and post to Instagram #MarkTheHoopster. Ask a friend to join you in the challenge and please send them a link to purchase the book: www.hoopsters.club/snipershandbook

Alas, my motive is ultimately *love*: love for God, love for others, and love of the game. I'm paying forward all my gift blessings with the fervent hope that they are abundant blessings to you in ways far beyond basketball.

Happy shooting. And don't forget to have *fun!* MJ

## Shot Improvement Pledge

_____

Signed, _____ Date: _____

"33" Average: _____ "33" Avg. After 45 days_____

## Shot Improvement Pledge

_____

Signed, _____ Date: _____

"33" Average: _____ "33" Avg. After 45 days_____

## Shot Improvement Pledge

_____

Signed, _____ Date: _____

"33" Average: _____ "33" Avg. After 45 days_____

# LAW 1: RIGHT FORM & MOTION (PHYSICS)

The first Law of Shooting Lethality is based on the laws of physics and details all the right forms and motions your body must conform to for maximum Lethal shooting power, accuracy, and efficiency. All the forms and motions are illustrated in the Lethal Shot Blueprint. In this section I will share the Blueprint followed by a thorough explanation of each form and motion as well as training recommendations.

By the end of this section you will know how to 1) build a fundamentally sound foundation to establish your center of gravity and straighten all your body lines; 2) load and transfer maximum energy from your feet to your wrist to shoot with ZERO DOUBT of failure with maximum power and accuracy. #ZeroDoubtLethality

## Lethal Shot Blueprint

> *"[To understand a new way of doing something], you must not only understand how it looks and feels; you must understand <u>how it works</u>."*
> — *Steve Jobs*

The Blueprint is the <u>design</u> of the Lethal Shot. A design is "a plan or drawing produced to show the look

27

and function of an object before it is built or made." The Blueprint is showing you the look and function of the shooting system before you build it into your shooting machine.

Since the Blueprint's graphics are well organized and easy to follow, it might be tempting to start rebuilding your jump shot by mimicking the forms and motions and skipping all my extra commentary. Resist the temptation. If you skip the commentary, you will hit a glass ceiling at some point. You must understand how the shot <u>works</u> before building it. It's not as simple as it appears.

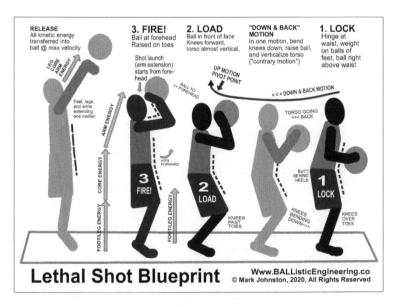

**Lethal Shot Blueprint**   Www.BALListicEngineering.co
© Mark Johnston, 2020, All Rights Reserved

Without further ado, starting right now, imagine your body as a vertical bow and the ball as an arrow. This "bow and arrow" state of mind is going to help you understand the kinetic and ballistic concepts in this book. If you haven't already, print the Blueprint out ASAP (see back of book for print-friendly version).

## Lethal Shot Blueprint: Three Forms, Two Motions

Think of the Lethal Blueprint as a short movie clip of the full jump shot and the mechanical drawings as freeze frames. Each of the figures in the Blueprint represent a single freeze frame of the shot. The black and gray figures labeled "Lock, Load, and Fire!" represent the beginning, middle, and end forms the body takes during the shot. The gray figures are reference points to show you what is happening in-between and after the main forms so you can understand the big picture.

In addition to the three main forms (Lock, Load, and Fire!) there are two main motions that *fuse* them together into one smooth, unified shot. The first motion is what I call the "down and back" motion that fuses the Lock and Load positions; the second motion is called the "up" motion, which fuses the Load and Fire! positions. You will need to learn all five forms and motions and fuse them together into one harmonious shooting machine. That will require both mind and body training.

29

Below I have included a summary of the three forms, two motions, and their purposes. Notice how each one shifts smoothly without disruption to the next, like the hits of a drum beat.

- **LOCK position** – the purpose is to establish a balanced and level *shooting foundation*, set your feet, lock in your center of gravity, and hinge your hips to shift to the…

  - o DOWN and BACK motion – the purpose is to set your shot into rhythmical motion, lower your body to jump, and raise ball to your head to shift to the…

- **LOAD position** – the purpose is to load maximum energy in your legs, glutes, hips, and arms, pivot between "down and back" motion and "up" motion, and aim the ball to shift to the…

  - o UP motion – the purpose is to uncoil all stored energy potential and transfer it upward from your feet to your legs to your core to your arms to shift to the…

- **FIRE! Position** – the purpose is to be in the perfect launch position <u>under</u> the ball to lift and fire the ball, snap your wrist, and release the ball at the perfect time before the apex of your jump.

## Lock, Load, Fire! #LoLoFi

All three forms and two motions occur sequentially, in one unified, undivided motion. Unity and harmony of all parts is the most important feature of the Lethal Shot that you must know and understand. Unity and harmony generate great power and accuracy.

> **Engineer's note:** Pay close attention to the "up motion shift" arrow in the blueprint; it is where the two contrary motions meet and must be smoothed into one. Just planting a seed for now. I will cover it in depth later.

Your first assignment is to burn these forms and motions into your mind and muscle memories (yes, both your mind and your body have "memory") and learn the exact movements you need to shift from one form to the next in one, undivided motion.

Understand this: motion, rhythm, and timing bring everything together into one harmonious, undivided, upward movement that has one purpose: to transfer as much balanced and direct kinetic energy into the ball and fire it in the most powerful and correct trajectory possible.

Remember, while I have broken down the shot into three forms and two motions so you can learn them, your goal is to ultimately fuse (or "smooth") them all into one repeatable movement. Just keep that in the back of your mind for now. At this knowledge gathering stage, no actual shooting practice is necessary. Again, this section all about gaining knowledge and understanding.

In the next section I cover all three forms and motions in detail, along with training instruction for each.

### *Blueprint Shot Form 1: The LOCK Position*

At the start of full shot, if time allows, the Sniper generally takes a quick stand in what I call the "Lock Position." In this position, he sets his *true* foundation and center of gravity with his weight slightly forward and evenly distributed between both legs. Though it is not always practical to lock in like this in a game situation, it is how you should practice and how you should set up whenever possible.

If nothing else, getting in the habit of securing the Lock position will get your mind and muscles used to establishing center of gravity, however quickly, before going into the shooting motion, which is <u>crucial</u> for several reasons I will be discussing shortly.

Notice how the Sniper's arms are forming "L" shapes, his feet are straight, aligned, and pointed a little to the left; his weight is on the balls of his feet (heels slightly lifted, but not much—sometimes more than others, depending on if he is taking a set shot or coming off a pick, step-back, etc.); and his head is up and looking at the front of the rim. Don't dismiss the importance of that last one. Many people look down or at the ball or defender when they shoot. Fix your eyes on the future prize! #EyesOnThePrize

A note about hinging at the waist. Hinging at the waist is different from bending over. To hinge at the waist, you rotate your pelvis like lowering for a deadlift. The "hinge" allows your butt to get back behind your heels which, you will see soon, is critically important. I will also cover this fully in the upcoming video demo.

Also, pay attention to the dashed line in front of the Sniper's hips showing his fairly sharp-angled body bend (if he is shooting super long distance, it is even sharper). Keep your eye on this dashed line in the subsequent images as it bends deeper and then straightens out as he goes through the shooting motion.

It's important to understand you do not jump and shoot from the Lock position. The Lock position is the gravity-centering form you take prior to making the "down and back" motion to the *Load* position (from where you will jump).

If you are used to shooting quickly without any sort of setup, you will need to change the way you *think* about preparing to shoot. Notably, you will need to shift from a "jump and shoot" thought pattern to a "set, jump, and shoot" thought pattern. The goal is to think: "set my feet and center of gravity then shoot" rather than "jump and shoot." There is a *huge* difference between those two thought patterns.

---

*Coach's note:* I have found people who don't have a lot of patience—myself included—find it difficult to get into the habit of setting their center of gravity prior to shooting. If you are impatient or tend to hurry a lot, you will need to learn to exercise patience and self-control like an archer. New radical thought to mediate on: **Patience is power.**

---

## A Sound Shooting Foundation

> *"If your foundation is crooked,*
> *your shot will be crooked." — Mark*
> *Johnston*

There are two important reasons you must train your mind and body to set a "sound foundation" in the Lock position: *to establish a balanced center of gravity* (which generates the most shooting power) and *truest possible lines* (which ensures the highest degree of shooting accuracy). Power, accuracy, and efficiency are the three ultimate goals of the Lethal shot, and they start with a sound foundation.

### Balanced Center of Gravity

Establishing a balanced center of gravity with your legs ensures your body will generate the most amount of upward power ("kinetic energy") to transfer into your core and arms to shoot. Don't believe me; believe the master teacher of physics, Sir Isaac Newton:

> *"A progressive motion (and the power it generates) starts with the center of gravity." — Isaac Newton*

Power starts with the center of gravity. Therefore, the more balanced your foundation center of gravity, the higher the probability of uninhibited and maximum energy transfer to the ball in every situation. That is a foundational LAW of physics you can fully believe and stand on without any doubt. I call it "Zero Doubt Shooting Confidence." #ZeroDoubt

### Truest Possible Lines

The second reason for setting a sound foundation is to get your body lines in the straightest angles most conducive to launching the most powerful shot. To that end, notice the Sniper's arms are in straight angles at his sides, he is hinged at the waist, his torso is tilted forward, and his lower back is straight. His whole body is in very straight, angled, symmetrical lines. Study these lines and remember them.

In summary, the more balanced and truer your foundation, the more optimally-positioned your body lines will be, and consequently the greater the probability you will launch the ball with maximum velocity and accuracy.

## About the Ball

Notice the Sniper's shooting hand is on the side of the ball (however, as he lifts the ball, he rotates it, so his shooting hand is more on top and ultimately under the ball — more on this later). Also notice how he's not holding the ball too low; it's between his belly button and his sternum and only must travel a short distance to his head level.

Why should you hold the ball up a little higher when you set up? Because the more you have to raise the ball to shoot, the more complicated and hard-to-control the shot becomes (not to mention it requires more energy). For that reason, you will be hearing a lot more about "getting your arms out of your shot" in the pages ahead.

## Lock Position Commentary

In practice, before games, and when taking set shots, the Sniper always starts his shot in the Lock position, although in games he's often in a hurry and can't form it fully. But even when he can't form it fully, he still sets his center of gravity and straightens his lines in mid-air. The reason he can do this is because his muscles *remember* from all his Lock position training what the correct lines *feel like* when he is in mid-air, and accordingly they shift into those lines. That is also how he can make off-balance shots.

I know the Lock position looks simple (and it is), but don't mistake simple for easy. It requires muscle memory and stabilization training. When I first started training, I thought I could just mimic it; but when I took a picture of myself, I wasn't even close! It has taken me a while to know by "feel" if I am in the right form—and I still get it wrong and must recalibrate now and then. I recommend having someone take a picture of you in what you *think* is the correct form and then compare it to the Blueprint.

> **Engineer's note:** *Calibration and recalibration is hugely important! The Blueprint needs to become your map and the mirror needs to become your compass to see if you're conforming to it. Recalibrate constantly. As my friend Dom says, "No discounts." Meaning no shortcuts or selling yourself short! #NoDiscounts*

When I set up in the Lock position, I focus on getting my feet planted and my body weight balanced equally on both feet, then hinging at the waist so my butt goes back and my knees bend a little, always ensuring the ball is above my waist. Note: I don't think like this in the middle of competition. In competition I play by feel and rely on muscle memory. This is why it is so crucial to get your mind and body locked into the "right" form and motion in practice: so, it is automatic in games.

A few more thoughts on hinging at the waist. To reiterate, hinging at the waist (which allows your butt to naturally shift back and your torso to lean forward) is different than simply bending over at the waist—in which case you bend at the lower back (ouch!) and your butt stays over your heels. Using your lower back to bend over is horrible for two reasons: First, it requires a massive amount of oxygen and energy to support your whole torso; second, it puts tremendous strain on your spine and makes you vulnerable to back muscle spasms and/or pinched nerves. You don't want either of those things as they will put you on the sidelines for weeks—if not months.

The correct way to bend over to shoot, to jump, or for deadlifts (which, along with dumbbell military press are arguably the most important strength exercise you can do for shooting), is to contract your abs, then hinge at the waist and rotate your pelvis back. Though your lower back will help hold your torso up, it won't be bent, and it won't have to work nearly as hard because your abs will be assisting. Your back will thank you!

As you hold the Lock position, notice you don't need to contract your abs to stay in it—but you should. The more you contract your abs, the less your lower back will have to help. You should be on the balls of your feet (and able to wiggle your toes—if you can't you are too far forward). Contracting your abs will also put in the best position to draw your hips forward (as you will need to do to shift to the Load position).

> **Coach's note:** Always contract your abs before bending over at the waist! Back injuries, especially sprains, are the worst and will sideline you for weeks! For that matter, engage your abs (and glutes!) whenever you are walking, running, jumping, shooting, or lifting.

**Lock Position Training**

To get into the Lock position, contract your abs, take one step forward, set your feet with weight on the balls of your feet, hinge at the waist, bend your knees slightly, make sure your forearms are parallel with ground, hold your head up, and then hold that position for about 10 seconds at least 20 times daily. If your lower back starts barking, that's a sign your core is weak, same with your other muscles. As you get stronger, you can and should hold this position with a medicine ball. This is called stabilization and muscle memory training.

> **Coach's note:** Don't just pump weights in the gym. Muscle stabilization, neuro-muscle memorization, and balance training are three of the greatest training secrets of becoming a lights-out shooter and much more.

Important! While you are set and fully balanced in the Lock position, remember when you're actually shooting you will hold it only for a split second to get centered and trued up to the basket. The only reason you hold it for ten seconds during training is to build the stabilizing muscles and get your body to memorize how it feels. Again, don't take this position for granted. Master it.

**Lock Position Summary**

The purpose of the Lock position is to take a stand, set and balance your center of gravity, your body lines *trued* up, hinge back, and prepare to shift perfectly to the Load position.

## *Blueprint Form 2: The LOAD Position*

The Load position serves three purposes: first, to "crouch" and load energy potential to jump and shoot (like pulling the arrow of a bow back); second, to shift or "pivot" from the "down and back" motion to the "up" motion; third to aim the ball. It can be thought of as the "crouch, pivot, aim" position.

KNEES PAST TOES

Remember when I said to think of your body as a bow and the ball as an arrow? Think of the Load position as the point where the arrow is pulled all the way back and ready to be released.

In the Load position, your hips should *almost* be all the way forward (notice the torso is not fully vertical yet in the Load position), you should feel your lower body weight leaning forward on your quads and Achilles and soleus muscles, and your upper body weight should be balanced on your pelvis over your heels with hardly any tension. You should be tightening/contracting your abs to stay upright. (Your abs should have already been contracted when you got into the Lock position).

The Load position is a very important position because it is the split-second launch pad where you load energy potential to transfer straight upward into the Fire! position to launch the ball. Remember, this is not a pause or hitch in the shot but rather what the body looks like when it is fully Loaded with energy potential and ready to launch.

Why did I choose this particular freeze frame for the Load position? Because, it is the exact mid-way point between the Lock and Fire positions, and therefore the **pivot point** where your body shifts from the **down and back motion** to the **up motion**. Read the previous line again. We will be talking about this critical pivot point again soon. Refer to the Blueprint right now and notice the "up motion pivot point" on it. That is where the transition from "down and back" motion to "up" motion takes place. I call it the "motion pivot point."

In the Load position, the Sniper's knees are forward, butt is over heels, torso is almost verticalized, the ball is at or just above head level, arms are in hard-angled V shapes and almost parallel with the ground, heels are lifted, and all weight is balanced on high balls of feet (although torso weight is balanced on a neutral pelvis and being held/stabilized by the flexed abs with no strain on lower back at all). Also, the Sniper's hand is now mostly under the ball.

The Load position is the launch pad to load energy and the split-second <u>pivot point</u> between the "back and down" motion and the "up" motion. I can't emphasize this enough: The split second the ball gets to your face (very close to it, in fact), you will be simultaneously rolling on the balls of your feet (without any pause) to jump and rise up into the Fire! position to shoot. It's a continuous motion.

The straighter and truer the lines of your body are in the Load position, the straighter and truer the ball will travel to the rim. Read that line again; it is of profound importance.

Remember, you are looking at a single freeze frame, NOT a hitch in the jump shot. The frame before this the Sniper was bending his knees to jump. The frame after this he is jumping. That should tell you how quickly this form comes and goes. Meditate on that a lot. The immediate movement after this is to rise UP to bring the ball to your forehead (the Fire! position) and launch it.

---

*Coach's note: True story: the more you try to aim and control the ball with your arms and shoulders, the more you will miss, I promise. The arms and hands are way to squirrely and hard to control to be trusted to be fully in charge of shooting. Stay tuned for the Shooter's Creed that will affirm this truth with some profound ancient wisdom!*

---

## Energy Loading

In the context of energy loading, the Load position reminds me of tiger's crouch before it explodes upward to jump. I always tell people, "Think: crouching tiger, hidden dragon." Why? The Load form stores up and hides serious power that unleashes a deadly, fire-breathing dragon from all over the floor! A true *killer!* Yes, I have a creative imagination. Have some fun with this. Get in the spirit and give yourself a *Lethal* nickname. It's a major confidence builder. Call me "Crouching Tiger, Hidden Dragon." ☺

## Weight Balance

In the Load position, your knees will be out in front of your feet and your torso will be sitting back, almost like sitting on a barstool. Your torso will be balanced and stabilized over your heels by your core muscles, and your whole body weight will be supported mostly by your core, quads, legs, and feet. You should feel the weight burden emphasis in your quads, not in your knees. Note: If you feel it in your knees, your quads will probably need to be strengthened.

To reiterate, the torso is held up (stabilized) and balanced by your core, mostly your abs (which you should have contracted in the Lock position). This is one of the biggest differences between the Lethal shot and other shots: since the torso is not tilted forward, it is being stablized more by the abs and hips than by the lower back. This position might feel weird and maybe even make your leg muscles (and even your knees and lower tailbone) sore at first; but in time your body will adapt to it, and soon you will start realizing its many

benefits—including no more sore lower and l
backs, more energy, more power, etc.

## Torso Talk: Simplicity is Power

 If the Load position is new to you, you
might encounter resistance from your mind
and body. Why? Because most of us have
been conditioned to believe that in order to
shoot the ball at the rim we must tilt at the
torso and make a forward jumping motion
from there—like the image on the left. Notice
the torso is tilted forward. That is what we naturally
want to do because the rim is of course in front of us. It
feels very awkward to actually shift our torso **back**
_before_ we jump up and shoot forward.

Many people don't verticalize their torso until during
or after the jump. In fact, some of the greatest players
don't straighten their torsos until they are launching to
jump or in mid-air. When we don't verticalize our torso
before jumping, we must use our torso and arms to
create most of the energy to shoot, which is not
efficient or reliable because the legs are way more
powerful and can generate way more energy.

Case in point. Notice the next image on the right.
The figure is actually a trace I did of one of the greatest
player's body before he pulled up for a jumper in the
Finals. Notice how his torso and arms are both

45

catapulting the ball forward using all upper body strength, rather than lifting it with lower-body-generated energy. This is very common and makes for a low trajectory shot. It's good for about 32% accuracy (potentially a little more IF you are a hall of famer). The truth is, he could have shot exponentially better had he verticalized his torso before he shot the ball.

Why? Because in order to transfer the kinetic energy generated from your feet, legs, and core into your arms to launch the ball in the most most vertically powerful and accurate (read: on target with a high arch) form possible, your torso cannot be tilted. If it is, you must verticalize it after you launch because you can't shoot with a nice high arch with a tilted torso. Try it. It's very difficult to execute. This speaks to the #CriticalityOfVerticality

Verticalizing your torso <u>after</u> launch is a serious mind, power, and accuracy drain. It turns your shot into a "two-motion" and "two-thought" shot rather than a one-motion and one-thought shot. It also forces the arms and shoulders to get way more involved, which leads to tension and aiming problems. It also saps your vertical energy transfer. Remember, simple is better. The less you have to do and think about, the better! Radical thought change: **simplicty is power.**

## About the Arms

Important to understand: from the Load position to the end of the shot no arm aiming is needed—which is a great gift of <u>simplicity</u> the Lethal design offers and a concept that it may take you a while to fully grasp.

If you are wondering how you will generate arm shooting power from this position, don't worry. Your arm shooting power is going to mostly come from your legs and core because in the split-second before you reach this position your feet and legs will already be starting to launch and providing upward kinetic energy to feed your arms.

## About the Hips

Notice in the Blueprint how the Sniper's pelvis never goes beyond level as he jumps (meaning he never thrusts his hips too far forward). This is noteworthy because when some people shoot, they thrust their pelvis/hips forward too much, which causes their torso to lean back, which is a major power drain and, like the torso tilt, is an opposing force that compromises the criticality of verticality for power and accuracy.

> *Coach's note:* Every single shot counts. Therefore, shooting even 1% better than everyone else is enough to win games (how many times have you seen a game come down to a single free throw?).

I encourage you to read this section and the previous one several times. Learn it, know it, understand it. Say these concepts out loud. Look up terms you aren't familiar with. Read articles on them. Became a hoops scientist. You need to retrain your body and mind to obey new laws they do not yet know. Obey your thirst? No. Quench your thirst, obey the laws of physics. #NewWay #NWOT

## Load Position Training

In order to train the Load position, I highly recommend starting in the Lock position, as seen in the graphic, and getting used to the "down and back" motion.

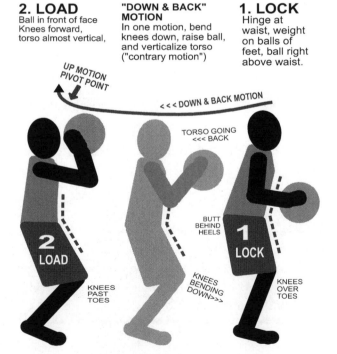

**2. LOAD**
Ball in front of face
Knees forward,
torso almost vertical,

**"DOWN & BACK"**
**MOTION**
In one motion, bend
knees down, raise ball,
and verticalize torso
("contrary motion")

**1. LOCK**
Hinge at
waist, weight
on balls of
feet, ball right
above waist.

UP MOTION
PIVOT POINT

<<< DOWN & BACK MOTION

TORSO GOING
<<< BACK

BUTT
BEHIND
HEELS

**2**
LOAD

**1**
LOCK

KNEES
PAST
TOES

KNEES
BENDING
DOWN>>>

KNEES
OVER
TOES

Here's how to do it: From the Lock position, lower your body slightly by bending your knees AND bringing your hips forward (which verticalizes your torso) WHILE raising the ball up and back to your head—all in one smooth motion. Now freeze and hold it for 5 seconds, balancing on the balls of your feet, and holding steady with your abs. Done! Check a mirror or video recording to see if you got it right. Do this 20 times a day at least.

Here's a tip to gauge if your "down and back" motion is correct. Have someone video record you from the side and watch what your head does. From the Lock position, if your head dips slightly forward (as you bend your knees) then straight back and slightly down, you're doing it right! If your head moves *up*, you're doing it wrong. By the way, some shooters slightly dip the ball first before raising it to generate rhythm.

If you have shifted from the Lock to the Load position perfectly, your body will be in the perfect form to—in the next split second—launch straight up into the Fire! position in the most explosive, efficient, and undivided manner possible. That is what I call "direct, exponential, vertical launch power."

**Load Position Training Insights**

- Lowering your body down while raising the ball up at the same time is called "contrary motion." New thought to ponder: contrary

49

motion. It might take a little while to wrap your mind around it.

- Don't get comfortable pausing in the Load position. Why? Because the instant before the ball is at head level you should already be starting the "UP" motion with your feet and legs. I'm only telling you to pause in it during training to learn and remember what it feels like.

- As you raise the ball to your head, make certain: 1) your forearm is closing the V into a harder angle; and 2) your shoulder is rotating to get your upper arm parallel with the ground. By the time the ball is at head level, your forearm should be almost parallel with the ground. I will be discussing this more in the upcoming video.

If you've never shot this way before, your knees, Achilles, calves, and quads might be sore because this is a very leg-centric shot. Your body will tell you what hurts, and you will have to do work to get flexible and strong in those muscular areas. I will discuss this more in the last section of the book. For now, go easy on yourself. The best things in life take time to develop, my friends. Patience is power.

> **Coach's note:** *About your abs. Always tighten/contract your abs when you are on the court for shooting, running, jumping, everything. Marathon runners run with their abs contracted! You can't do enough front and side planks. Your back will thank you.*

Don't get discouraged if your "down and back" shift from Lock to Load (or holding Load) feels unnatural, painful, or awkward. These are normal responses to learning a completely new movement like this, especially one with contrary motion. It is also quite possible that you will need to do some strengthening and stretching work to get symmetrically strong and limber. Don't rush it. Get strong, don't get injured,

## The 'Down and Back" Motion

The "down and back" motion between Lock and Load positions is one of the most important components of the Lethal shot. The purpose of it is to: 1) <u>verticalize the torso; and 2) create rhythm and energy potential to jump and shoot</u>. Don't worry if you're still not fully tracking. I will be demonstrating in the upcoming video.

For now, just remember the shift from Lock to Load enables you to get your torso straight with your knees bent so you can blast upward, straight upward, without having to worry about verticalizing your torso during the jump motion (which causes all kinds of tension, power loss, instability, and other problems).

As for me, as I was learning the "down and back" motion, it raged against my natural tendencies and felt awkward. I had to train and <u>retrain</u> my body to do it. Now I exaggerate it a lot when warming up just to get the "groove" of it. Keep in mind it's not just a motion to get in the right position; it's a move that generates rhythm and power to feed directly into the jump shot. It's all one smooth motion. You'll get it in time, don't worry.

> *Coach's note:* For the record, my calves, knees, and lower back got sore from shifting from the Ready to Aim position a lot. Those were indications I needed to strengthen those areas. Always, LISTEN TO YOUR BODY. Your body is smart, and it will signal you when there is a problem. Do not ignore it! By the way, I RARELY exercise muscles that are sore. I let them heal!

## Load Position Summary

In summary, the main reason the Sniper positions his body in the Load form is to load all the energy potential into his powerful legs, hips, and glutes and get his torso vertical so all he has to do from there is <u>simply</u> jump straight up and shoot to release the energy. This "trued up," verticalized position ensures there will be no opposing forces from his lower back, arms, shoulders, etc. to introduce tension or imbalance and slow the kinetic energy transfer from legs to wrist.

Since every part of the body is moving when shifting from the Lock to the Load position, initially it's hard to determine what to focus on. I've learned it's best to first focus on the movement of my feet and legs since they are generating all the energy I will shoot with, then my arms.

So, we've set up in the Lock position with the waist hinge, we've grooved to the Load position with the "down and back" motion to crouch and store up kinetic energy, and now it's time to actually Fire! the ball!

*Coach's note: If you are very astute you may have noticed the Lock and Load positions are almost exactly how great snipers shoot free throws too. This is not a coincidence. You can and should use the whole shooting motion to shoot free throws too.*

### Form 3: Fire! Position

The third and final form of the Lethal Blueprint is the Fire! position. This is the form the Sniper's body is in the split second before firing the ball. If all else fails, and he is unable to get into the Lock or even Load position, he almost always ensures he locks this form before shooting.

Technically, you can skip Lock and Load and shoot from the Fire! position. Though it requires way more jump and arm power, it's still more effective than shot types that start with a tilted torso. I still shoot from this form all the time, especially when a defender is reaching. In time you will be able to fire from Load or Fire or positions in between. The Lethal shot lends itself to all situations.

The first thing you might notice is that the Fire! position is very similar to the Load position. Can you tell the difference between the two? The only things that have changed from the Load to the Fire! positions are: 1) He has raised the ball to his forehead, which many people refer to as the "set point"; 2) he has straightened out his legs more, raised up on his toes more, and brought his hips forward more.

Notice the hard-angled "V" shape of his arms is still locked in. Also notice his hand is under the ball and over his shoulder. This is made possible due to his right shoulder being raised so his upper arm can point upward towards the basket. Read that last line again. It will come back to haunt you if you don't understand it.

The most important thing I can say about the Fire! position is that all the previous motions have put his body in the perfect position *under the ball* to *lift it up* at a high angle towards the basket to generate a powerful, high-arching, accurate shot.

So, let's make sure we are clear on all this. In the Load position the Sniper crouched and got ready to shoot; then, from there, he simultaneously rose up on his toes, extended his legs, and raised (more like *lifted*) the ball to his forehead to shoot. From this Fire! position, the Sniper is using the generated upward energy from his feet, legs, and core to launch the ball, which enables him to extend his arms in a nice, smooth, single "stroke" that doesn't require a massive amount of arm strength.

The less power your arms have to generate, the easier it is to shoot the ball in a very straight line that does not require a lot of wobbly arm controlling and aiming. That's not to diminish the importance of the arms. You will need to develop a smooth and perfect extension, and I recommend working on doing just that as often as possible.

The most noteworthy thing about the Sniper's Fire! form is his extreme vertical position, which is only made possible due to his verticalized torso and almost fully neutral pelvis alignment from when he was in the Load position. The perfect Load position allows him to <u>blast straight upward</u> with all his V-stored energy potential right through the Fire! position without any other mind or body distractions and make a simple shooting arm extension. Simplicity is truly a beautiful thing. Visualize the Lethal shot being a very vertically-oriented shot in every way.

> *"Simple is harder than complex. You have to work hard to get your thinking clean to make something simple. But it's worth it in the end because once you get there, you can move mountains." — Steve Jobs*

The vertical kinetic energy blast from transferring all the energy potential stored in his legs and core to his arms at the perfect time does two primary things: First, it creates tremendous upward force (which makes it possible to shoot from NBA three range with only a tiny jump off the ground!); and second, it encourages a lifting motion with the shooting arm rather than a throwing motion, which results in a higher shot trajectory and thus higher rate of accuracy.

From the Load to the Fire! position, the Sniper's feet, legs, arms, body uncoil in perfect harmony and timing. As he rises upward, the split second the ball gets to his forehead he fires the ball right before the top of his jump. It's one, smooth motion all the way through to his hard wrist snap:

*Lock, Load, Fire* in one smooth motion.

The result is a high-arching loft with great back spin that has a tremendous chance of going in, even if it's slightly left or right or short or long!

That said, as I alluded to previously, don't make the mistake of thinking the Lethal shot is comprised of different movements/stages/phases. Though it might seem that way because I have shared three different snapshots of it, that's not the case at all. The down and back motion is also creating kinetic energy and rhythm to jump. All the rhythm and energy go directly UP into the jump and shot.

---

**Coach's note:** Back spin creates more than just pretty swishes; it also helps create "loft," which is that beautiful floating quality when the ball seems to magically hang in the air briefly before it splashes through the net. Don't you just love that?? ☺ -MJ

---

## Fire! Position Training

The best way to practice the Fire! position is by doing the Lock and Load forms first and powering right into it with a smooth transition. Have a look at the Blueprint again and burn it in your memory.

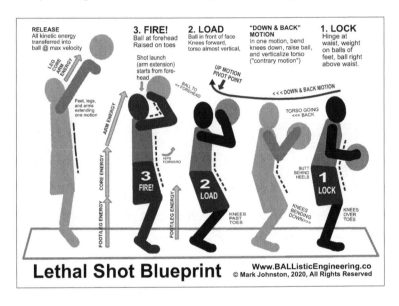

**Lethal Shot Blueprint**   Www.BALListicEngineering.co
© Mark Johnston, 2020, All Rights Reserved

Notice what happens between the Load and Fire! forms. With his abs still contracted to keep his torso verticalized, he rises on his toes, extends his legs, which brings his hips the rest of the way forward, and he raises the ball to his forehead to shoot in one unified, harmonious motion. After extending his arm to shoot, he releases the ball just as he leaves the ground and before he reaches the apex of his jump. By the time he releases the ball, his torso and legs are straight, his pelvis is neutral, and his arms are extended.

Practice the whole Blueprint simultaneously at home in one smooth motion with just a tiny jump making sure to unbend your arms and legs simultaneously while rising on to your tip toes all the way through to a powerful snap of your wrist to loft the ball upward. Do it without the ball at first and just visualize. Watch yourself in a mirror too.

Once you get the basic motion right, practice with a ball, then take it to the court and start working it out. Don't "aim" the ball as you shoot! One of the purposes of the Load position is to position the ball in front of your face and aim.

In other words, in the Load position, you will have already drawn the arrow back and aimed it at the target. Now it's just a matter of letting it go in the most simple, direct, undivided, and well-timed motion as possible. As a matter of fact, you will be aiming the ball in the Lock position. It saves you the complicated trouble of trying to aim after you launch. It's a new way of thinking about shooting so let it sink. #NWOT

To reiterate, don't let your arms control the shot. Shoot it first with your legs, then your core, then your arms, and finally your wrist— having *zero doubt* that your foundation (Lock) and launch pad (Load and Fire!)

lines are true and reliable. Never try to push or control the ball with your arms. The great hoops Sniper is more like an archer than a quarterback.

*"The one who doubts is double-minded (divided) and unstable in all his ways."* — St. James

## Step by Step Instruction

Start practicing by shooting from 6 FEET away from the front of the rim to lock in mechanics. The ball should swish and roll back to you if you are nailing it. Once a month I video record my profile as I shoot from six feet away to make sure my form is correct. Move back to the free throw line and elbows as you improve.

As you get better, start shooting from short and mid-range taking just a little tiny jump. If you're doing it right, you will be transferring energy very efficiently and will find you barely have to jump to shoot. And even the shots that come up short or left and right will still rattle or roll in (which is why as a coach I focus more on misses than makes—more on that in a future post).

As you start draining the short and mid-range shots, shoot from further and further out, being very careful to maintain your form. If you have to break your form to shoot, you are either not transferring energy efficiently (more on that in the next section), or you are not yet strong enough for the distance you're trying to shoot from. We haven't got into strength yet (it deserves its own book), but I will be covering it soon.

As you shoot, think of creating rhythm through the "down and back" motion between Lock and Load so you can transfer maximum kinetic energy in your legs to transfer upward to your arms. Visualize and feel transferring energy from your feet all the way to your wrist snap to create spin energy, always making sure to let go of the ball slightly before your reach the top of your jump for maximum power.

Congratulations, you have learned the Lethal jump shot design! Now it's just a matter of practicing wisely and methodically to master LEVEL 1 LETHALITY.

## Form and Motion Summary

In summary, the Lethal shot is all about taking a stand in the Lock form to center your gravity on a solid foundation that won't shift under you, grooving smoothly into the Load form, launching upwards with your feet, legs, and hips into the Fire! form, then releasing the ball with a full *pop* of the wrist before you reach the apex of your jump.

To reiterate, the five forms and motions of the Lethal shot do not happen in a mechanical, choppy way. In fact, to the naked eye, you can't perceive them. In full motion, the shot is just one, smooth motion: *boom-*

*boom-boom.* Listen closely to this: once you have the forms and motions mastered, you won't even think of them in steps. You will just have ONE, smooth shot with all three parts in harmony like three piano keys forming a TRIAD chord in music.

After analyzing, experimenting, and journaling for many years, I have concluded the Lethal Jumper design and its three *Lock, Load, Fire* forms and two motions you've learned are critical to developing a powerful, efficient, reliable, consistent, and correctly "arched" loft that is most conducive to getting the ball in the rim—which is the goal of basketball.

> **Coach's note:** *Practice and play. One thing's for sure, when you are actually playing, you can't think of the three forms at all; you just have to shoot by feel. Working on form and mechanics only happens in practice. More on this in the last section.*

All that said, while you can and will raise your shot percentage just by adhering to the Blueprint's five forms and motions, if you stay committed to improving, you will find—like I did—that you'll once again hit a glass ceiling and not be able to get beyond it. Why? Because there are still two more important laws and upgrades you need to add to your arsenal. The next section (Law #2: Right Mind State) is going to move you a quantum step closer.

Though you are free to keep reading, I recommend being able to shoot the Lethal shot correctly and consistently before moving on to the next law.

> **Engineer's Note:** *One more thing. I would recommend reading this book twice. It is deep and there is a lot to know and understand. Just keep seeking, and you will keep finding. That is also a law of the universe.* ☺
> *#SeekAndFind*

# LAW 2: RIGHT MIND STATE

*"Be transformed by the renewing of your mind..."* — St. Paul

Congratulations for making it to this point. You have already gained enough physics knowledge to transform your shooting machine into a powerful and accurate Lethal weapon on the court. If you've understood and applied all the knowledge and wisdom I've shared so far, you are considered a Level 1 Sniper, and I'm certain you've already seen major improvement in your shot. Good on you! Now it's time to learn the next transformational law of Lethal shooting, and that is the law of *mind power*.

In the first part of this section I will provide an overview of what "right" mind state is and why it's important, then I will discuss how mind state plays a role on the basketball court (through my own experiences to make it easy to understand), then I will share some mind state recommendations to achieve a "breakthrough" mind state.

# Mind State and Beliefs

*"Don't mistake the limits of your own mind for the limits of the universe." — Mark Johnston*

## Overview

Developing the "right" mind state is every bit as important to your shooting success as developing the right physical state. Notice I didn't say "mindset." Mindset is all the rage these days, but I don't find it helpful because the mind is never technically "set." The mind is always in motion, one way or another—even if it is stuck in a cycle. In fact, everything in the universe is in motion. More importantly, mindset is not belief-oriented, and without beliefs it is pointless to talk about the mind because our thoughts filter through our beliefs.

Mind state refers to the *condition* of your mind at any given time. What do I mean by condition? I'm referring to the overall condition of your mind (Peaceful? Anxious? Fearful?) and what you *believe*. Beliefs are things you accept to be TRUE. Beliefs are formed by the knowledge you gather through experience, observation, and spiritual revelation. Your beliefs are your truths. Collectively all your beliefs form your *reality* and dictate, yes dictate, how you view yourself versus others, how you view the world, and how you make decisions of all sorts—even on the basketball court when pulling up to shoot.

To say your beliefs are tyrannical is an understatement; they *dominate* your thoughts and dictate your choices about people, friends, spouses, food, jobs, and much more. For example, if you believe people are mostly untrustworthy, you will conduct your whole life that way; if you think people are mostly trustworthy you will conduct your whole life another way. If you believe you were born to succeed, you will make choices to succeed; if you believe you were born to fail, you will make choices to fail. You get the idea.

From everything you've read so far, you can rest assured your mind state and beliefs are related to each other, incredibly powerful, and absolutely play an integral performance role every moment of your life. This can be a good or bad thing depending on what kind of mind state and beliefs you have.

### Two Types of Mind States and Beliefs

30+ years of experience as a U.S. Army military intelligence soldier, business change leader, and trainer in the technology industry informs me people generally have one of two mind states: a limited mind state or an unlimited (or "breakthrough") mind state.

- **A limited (or "breakdown") mind state** is filled with limiting beliefs that prevent people from realizing their potential. These people are generally followers, skeptics, cynics, scoffers, doubters, jokesters, and disbelievers. These are the people who told Thomas Edison he was a fool to think he could channel electricity into a light bulb and illuminate the world at night.

- **An unlimited (or "breakthrough") mind state** is filled with limitless beliefs that lead to "breakthrough" discoveries, innovations, and quantum personal improvement. These people are generally leaders, optimists, artists, innovators, creators of all sorts, and generally encouraging and very curious about everything. These are people like Thomas Edison, Isaac Newton, Michael Jordan, Steve Jobs, Steph Curry, Elon Musk, and many others.

Question: Which type of mind state do you have? Probably goes without saying, but an unlimited "breakthrough" mind state is the *right* mind state for becoming a Lethal 3 Sniper.

Breaking news: Most people don't have an unlimited (or "breakthrough") mind state. Most people have limited mind states and limiting beliefs and consequently can't see beyond the limitations of the past and the present. Therefore, they get stuck in life and can't move forward. Many of them blame others for their lack of progress, but at the end of the day their own limiting beliefs keep them grounded. It doesn't have to be this way; we have the power to change our mind states and thus our futures.

## Changing Your Mind State

Good news! If you have a limited mind state, you can and will transform it to an unlimited "breakthrough" mind state, shatter glass ceilings, and become a record breaker IF you are committed and devoted to gaining knowledge and applying it to your life in every way. What kind of knowledge? Reality knowledge. Truth. The truth will make you FREE to soar on wings like an eagle. That is a Biblical and scientific fact.

What kind of truth? When it comes to basketball shooting, I'm referring to the truth about physics, truth about your unlimited potential, truth about the amazing future that awaits you IF you will just start looking to the future and believing in future possibilities rather than looking to the past and present and fixating on limitations.

Here's the deal: The more truth you learn and understand, the more your limiting beliefs will be replaced by limitless beliefs and the more FREE you will be to learn, grow, create, and set new records. In time, your whole "worldview" will totally change from a grounded and caged one to a totally FREE one that is no longer held captive under invisible glass ceilings.

How do I know this? Because it happened to me and I've seen it happen to many others. That's why in the next section I am going to explain the "breakthrough" mind state through my own real testimony about how my mind was renewed and changed from limited to unlimited. My hope is that you believe it and embark on your own journey to truth and freedom.

Before reading this, do another #CleanSlate and get ready for some serious transformation! #Breakthrough #NewWayOfThinking #NWOT

# How My Mind State Was Changed

### Backyard Battles

Let's start here: I didn't play hoops in high school or college. I wasn't even that coordinated as a kid. I rode BMX and avoided the basketball court—at least the formal one. But my dad Fred played in a local men's league, and me and my brother Eric battled non-stop on our backyard basketball court in Lake Tahoe, CA. I was Bird with my long-range bombs, my brother was Magic with what he called his "hook shot hot shot." Lord knows neither of us knew how to shoot correctly, but man did we have fun and dream big. My love for basketball was never really about winning. I just loved playing, watching, and analyzing hoops.

After high school I joined the U.S. Army. There I encountered some of the best street ballers in the country from every state! Those guys made me better, and I practiced relentlessly to compete with them. By the time I got out of the military I could play with just about anyone—even though I was still quite scrappy.

### Glass Ceiling

After the military, I played ball everywhere and was a good, but mostly streaky, shooter. I studied other shooters, I tried to emulate their mechanics, I lifted weights and practiced shooting for many hours (and suffered many injuries—especially my back), but no matter what I did, I could not significantly increase my field goal percentage in a game. I hit a "glass ceiling" and had no idea how to get beyond it.

> *"A glass ceiling is an invisible barrier that blocks you from rising any higher. The maddening part is you know it's there, but you don't know what's causing it." — Mark Johnston*

Even though I was a good player by some standards, I often couldn't hit shots in high-intensity games, especially when I needed to come from behind… or when I was just one shot away from winning the game and couldn't close it out. I also was vulnerable to "trash talk" and guys could easily take me out of my game with their mere words.

In time, hoops became more of a chore and a grind than a joy. Failing to improve with more practice, I grew weary, lost hope, and started assuming I just wasn't cut out for basketball. I wouldn't find out until much later that I was grounded not by my fate, or genetics, or lack of natural talent, or anything of the sort; I was grounded by two things: <u>my lack of knowledge and my limiting beliefs</u>.

### *Turning Point (Breakthrough Mindset)*

> *"There is no better time than the present moment to plant a new tree." — Mark Johnston*

But then one day, I read a pivotal and inspiring fitness article by a trainer who said the key to improving your performance in <u>anything</u> is not mere repetition and passionate intensity but "acquiring knowledge, practicing the right things right, and perseverance." In order to practice the right things right, he said, you must acquire knowledge, experiment with different adjustments, track your progress, keep what produces good results, throw out what doesn't produce good

results, and persevere until you get over the obstacle."
That is when I started thinking about having a
#Breakthrough state of mind.

From that point on I started questioning my beliefs,
especially ones about my potential. Soon, I realized
that due to childhood experiences (I will save those for
another time) I was skeptical, insecure (low self-worth),
and didn't have much hope in the future at all. In many
ways I was still bound to the past and the present
moment and couldn't see beyond them. I started
reading books by positive thinking as well as those by
futurists and inventors. I then came across the story of
a man I only knew a little about named Thomas Edison.

Edison is one of the greatest inventors of all time
who—through his learning, experiments, journaling,
and persistence—finally had a breakthrough when he
figured out how to channel electricity into a light bulb—
even when everyone told him it could NEVER be done.
I was really inspired by his future vision and
perseverance and started to believe I could have the
same state of mind about any of my own passions if I
changed my thought patterns. Then I saw a quote from
Edison that pushed me past my last mental obstacle:

*"There's a better way. Find it."*
*— Thomas Edison*

My jaw fell open when I read those words because it
hit me that no matter how good something is, and no

matter how much people believe there is no better solution, anything on earth CAN be improved—IF you are a SEEKER of knowledge and understanding AND you remain committed and <u>devoted</u> to a breakthrough.

This was a major turning point in my journey that inspired me to make a commitment to improve my jump shot—no matter what it took. It also inspired me to adopt what I call a *Breakthrough Mind State.* #NewWayOfThinking #NWOT

The more I researched, the more I found all the great inventors and leaders I admired had #Breakthrough mind states. Moses, Jesus, Isaac Newton, Einstein, Lincoln, Ben Franklin, Thomas Edison, MLK, etc. (not to mention all my favorite musicians like Gershwin, Led Zeppelin, Steely Dan, Pink Floyd, etc.) weren't grounded by limiting beliefs; they were always acquiring *new knowledge* and looking beyond the past and present to the future. And that's how they could see further and do things others couldn't do.

Bottom line: If you are going to be a fully Lethal Sniper, you will need to be a leader and have a #breakthrough mind state too. Yes, it will take some time to learn how, but it WILL come if you stay committed and devoted. I am proof.

## Commitment and Devotion to Continuous Improvement

*"You need devotion..."* — Earth,
*Wind, and Fire*

As the wise man says, every path to victory starts with a single step. I took the first step of my new journey by starting a notepad in Evernote called "Sniper Journal." My first note was my commitment and devotion to improving my shot. I then joined a gym and started going super early, before the crowd got there, and journaling a little after every session.

That would turn out to be a life-changing decision— and not just in terms of hoops. In no time it became a six-day-a-week habit, and everyone at the gym came to know me as the "basketball guy." One guy referred to me as "Mark the Hoopster." By the end of the year, I was 45 years old and easily one of the most devoted and fit people in the gym—even though my jump shot was still not even close to what it would become.

Oh, I should note that during this same time I was undergoing a spiritual awakening in which I was learning life, love, happiness, etc. wasn't about keeping my gifts for myself but rather sharing them with others (ask me about "Who do you play for?" if you want to know more—it's a mind-bending and life-changing truth). The seed had been planted that I would one day eventually share everything I had learned about shooting for the enjoyment of others. That was one of the main reasons I started journaling everything.

*"It is far better to give than receive." — St. Paul*

I was overjoyed to learn the liberating TRUTH that my purpose was to keep learning, growing, and improving in every way and paying it forward, and the only thing that could stop me was lack of knowledge and my own state of mind, both of which I had the power to control. It was my biggest "breakthrough" to date, and I haven't stopped learning and "breaking through" barriers since that day.

All that said, I couldn't have kept advancing (nor would I have been able to Blueprint the Lethal shot and write this book) had I not surrendered to the reality that regardless of my style, identity, wisdom, and experience, there was an objective truth called "physics" that trumped all those things, and unless I learned it and obeyed it, I was going to keep hitting glass ceilings. I had to accept there was an objective and absolute truth outside of my own ego that was bigger than me. And you will have to accept it too if you want to keep advancing in freedom and power.

# Gaining a Right Mind State

*"Our doubts are traitors and rob us of victory." — William Shakespeare*

### Truth Foundation

Let's start here: Just as the Lethal shot requires setting a solid physical foundation, it also requires setting a solid belief foundation, which is critical for shooting confidence and harmony between mind and body.

As I said at the end of the last section, setting a solid belief foundation requires we accept there is objective truth outside of us. In the case of shooting, the truth is called *physics*. And within physics there are laws, and the laws govern your body and the basketball every second you are on the court. Just because you don't know and/or believe the laws, doesn't mean they don't exist. The sooner you *believe* they exist, the sooner you will find that when the laws are obeyed (according to the Blueprint in Law #1), you can achieve far more than you or anyone else ever imagined possible.

New thought to ponder: Despite what cultural forces say, there is absolute truth, and the closer you get to it, the more powerful, accurate, and efficient you will become—on the court and off. As you become more established and rooted in irrefutable knowledge, you will become more confident. Then, when the game is on the line, and you're pulling up to shoot, rather than launching from a foundation of someone's uninformed and uncertain opinion (remember Frank Gamble — RIP!), you will be launching from a foundation of evidence-based, unshifting LAW, fully assured it will not shift like the shadows. #SoundFoundation #NWOT

### New Way of Thinking #NWOT

Now that you have hopefully accepted there are truths outside of you and you must learn and obey them for maximum success, I will share some insights regarding how a "breakthrough" state of mind thinks and operates. This is, by all means, a "new way of thinking," so don't be surprised if your own mind resists it. Don't mistake your mind's resistance for falsehood. Give it some thought. Mediate on it. It may take some time to grasp.

We can look to golfers to see "breakthrough" state of minds in action. Golfers seem to have a much higher awareness and appreciation for scientific knowledge/truth. You will rarely hear a golfer dismissing golf swing science. Watch golf swing analysis videos and read the comments. Many golfers are humble students of science and they love chasing the perfect swing. Hoopsters can learn a lot from them.

It's no coincidence that the greatest NBA shooter of all time is also an excellent golfer.

Here's a *truth bomb* about adopting the right mind state: if you seek to truly understand and apply the knowledge you've acquired, you can and will make real and measurable progress, you will be free to create, innovate, and enjoy the game, and you will share your gifts and make a positive difference in the world. That's the essence of Edison's quote: "There's a better way. Find it." I now live by that breakthrough-oriented proverb and it has enabled me to create and develop many software apps, songs, screenplays, and yes, a Lethal jump shot. It works!

Need more proof? Just think: If Henry Ford had a fixed mind state we'd still be riding around in horse and buggies! The same can be said for Steve Jobs and the iPhone. With every single new great product, someone who was open to change looked at an existing thing and said, "I can improve that" and victory followed. I'm encouraging you to evaluate every single basketball player (especially yourself) with the same *breakthrough* mind state that all the great innovators and leaders have had—and that is a mind state based on belief in truth and thoughts centered around possibilities rather than limitations.

## Fighting the Resistance

*"Great spirits have always encountered violent opposition from mediocre minds. The mediocre mind is incapable of understanding the man who [dares to think differently than the masses]."* — *Einstein*

If you are determined to change your mind state from limited to unlimited so you too can be FREE to innovate, break glass ceilings and records, and soar, you will be facing major resistance. From who? First from your own mind then, as you crush your limiting beliefs and start paying your knowledge forward, from other minds. It's important to understand the nature of the resistance so you can overcome it. Here are some insights that will better prepare you to recognize limiting beliefs (especially your own) and conquer them.

Through my experience and research, I've learned the limited mind state problem starts with the fact that most people (including me) were never taught how to shoot the ball correctly because we either didn't have a teacher or our teacher was an athlete or coach with zero scientific knowledge. And to be clear so there is no mistake, when I say 'correctly,' I'm talking about evidence-based, scientific truth regarding physics, energy transfer, release timing, range of motion, rhythm, and more. It seems these laws are alien to most hoopster minds, which is why they often respond with surprise or cynicism when they hear it.

Case in point. I can't tell you how many comments I see on YouTube shot analysis videos from naysayers such as, "This is junk science, just shoot the dang ball!" and "This scientific stuff is dumb, you can learn just by watching other shooters." Not coincidentally, these are the same low-info people who will never shoot better than 30% or less—especially when someone's hand is in their face.

When it comes to shooting the basketball, I've found the vast majority of minds (including my own at one point) have adopted a lot of *limiting beliefs* about shooting. One example is the popular limiting belief that shooting better than about 35-40% field goal percentage is prodigy-like and out of the reach of mere mortals like me and you. Another example is the low-info limiting belief that prevents people from surpassing those numbers.

Limiting beliefs such as these have profound performance consequences on the court and they are all *toxic* to your progress as a shooter. Why are limiting beliefs so dangerous? Because when you believe there is a "glass ceiling" of some sort preventing you from rising any higher, you will lack confidence (also known as "faith") in yourself, and your mind will instruct your body it is not capable of doing the very thing you are trying to do. This principle applies to anything in life, by the way.

For instance, while you are coaching yourself to "shoot the lights out" in the upcoming game, your doubtful limiting belief that only prodigies shoot above 40% whispers back to you, "Nope. You aren't a prodigy. It will never happen." In that case, you will be double-minded, and your indecisiveness will be projected to your body when you pull up to shoot. Rather than shoot boldly and decisively with assurance of a Lethal Level 3 Sniper, you will shoot tentatively like Frank Gamble and the probability of missing the shot will increase greatly. And you won't shoot better than 40%. In fact, you will be lucky if you shoot 30%.

Consequently, no matter how much time you spend mastering Law #1, if you don't get your mind state right and overcome your limiting beliefs, you will eventually hit a glass ceiling and not be able to move beyond it. This is not opinion; this is scientifically and Biblically supported fact.

How can you avoid having a limited mind state and adopt the right mind state? For that matter, what exactly is the right mind state? Here is the Biblical and scientific truth: "My people are destroyed for lack of knowledge" (Hosea 4:4). When you truly come to understand that, it will liberate you. And again, "knowledge" refers to TRUTH. Reality. As I said previously, you must shoot from a foundation of TRUTH to have full confidence in your shot. Without truth to stand on, your mind will resist and doubt, your mind and body will be divided when you shoot, and your shot will be more like a gamble than a confident shot. Remember Frank Gamble. RIP!

The main point I want to make here is that due to the widespread resistance to science and truth in hoops, I know from my own experience that even after you make a commitment to improve your jump shot and start applying the knowledge in this book, your mind and other minds you encounter will keep resisting the idea that there is a "right" way to shoot. Lethal shooting is a revolutionary idea and limited minds don't like revolutions because they require change, and people (including you and me) often fear change.

For all these reasons and more, you will need to fight through the internal and external resistance you experience and convince your mind with positive affirmations and perseverance that the *new way to shoot* is a true and good thing that will benefit you. Long story short: fight the change resistance with everything you've got! The best way to do that is arming yourself with as much knowledge as possible, striving to understand it, and changing your mind so your body will follow.

Believe this: You can and will overcome your own limited mind state and adopt an innovative, growth-oriented, limitless, evolutionary, breakthrough mind state that is not influenced by statistics, genetics, naysayers, scoffers, doubters, and blind sheep. With devotion (you need devotion), your mind and body will no longer strive for ordinary or sub-ordinary results but extraordinary results… with great confidence and assurance... with great faith… every time you pull up to shoot. Speaking of faith…

# 12 Breakthrough Affirmations

*"You have power over your mind. When you accept this, you will find strength." — Marcus Aurelius*

As you have read, your mind is profoundly powerful, and its limiting beliefs will dominate your life… if you LET THEM. Fortunately, as St. Paul says in the first quote of this section, your mind can be *renewed,* and your thought patterns can be changed. Yes, you can overcome your own self-limiting beliefs and, furthermore, replace them with unlimited beliefs to form a right state of mind conducive to explosive improvement and exponential gains.

So, how do you renew your mind and adopt a new set of unlimited beliefs to override your limiting beliefs and form a breakthrough mind state? First you must define your beliefs then you must start practicing them in every way.

Here is a short list of 12 "breakthrough" affirmations you can and should start saying to yourself frequently to drown out your limiting beliefs and develop a "breakthrough" mind state. I recommend putting these on little cards and taking them with you wherever you go. Of course, you can also develop your own. These are just suggestions.

"I believe I have unlimited potential and I will be victorious."

"I believe knowledge, commitment, devotion, perseverance, and practicing the right things right are the keys to victory."

"I believe the quality of practice is way more important than the quantity of practice."

"I believe in the laws of physics, and I believe they totally override anyone's personal opinion about shooting or basketball."

"I believe I can shoot 100% from the floor against anyone if my form, motion, mind, and body are right and harmonious."

"I believe the only thing that can prevent me from continuously improving is my own lack of knowledge and failure to remain committed and devoted."

"I believe anything is possible. Just because I can't see or comprehend something right now doesn't mean it's impossible."

"I believe I am a blessed, gifted person with unlimited potential who can never fail. There are no fails or setbacks, only learning and continuous improvement."

"I believe fear is the result of ignorance. Therefore, when I fear something, I will seek knowledge to understand what I am lacking so I can overcome it."

"I believe my mind and body must be harmonious, healthy, and undivided. Therefore, I will seek understanding and peace at all times."

"I believe with all my heart and mind and spirit that I will be a Lethal shooter and break all kinds of records."

"I believe in paying it forward, so I will always focus not on winning and being better than others, but on learning and growing so I can help others learn and grow."

#NWOT

# Mind State Summary

*"The people who are crazy enough to think they can change the world are the ones who do."*
— Steve Jobs

I know I covered a lot of information in this section, and I recognize it might be overwhelming. Take a breath. Soak it in and meditate on it before you make any judgments. See what the Spirit of life and truth reveals to you.

That said, if I have succeeded at making you feel uncomfortable, you're progressing! Yes, great change always starts with discomfort. No pain, no gain. Make no mistake, this book is not designed to make you feel comfortable, validate you, or re-teach you things you already know. It's designed to challenge your thinking so you can *breakthrough* old thought patterns and limiting beliefs that are BLOCKING you from seeing the possibilities and realizing your full God-gifted potential to soar to new heights like an eagle and break records. Whose records? Your records and any other records you set your sights on.

New way of thinking: discomfort when learning is a GOOD thing is a good thing and will yield GOOD results.

The whole point of adopting the right "breakthrough" mind state is to overpower the resistance to change in our minds. If you want to be a Level 2 (let alone 3) Lethal Sniper, you must get control of your mind; if you don't, IT WILL CONTROL (and defeat) YOU. That is not an opinion, that is a fact. In order to change it, you must get knowledge and understanding, change your way of thinking, and apply it every time you step on the court.

How serious are you about rising above the herd? I don't know about you, but I don't want the same old results. I assume you don't either since you bought this book. Good on you! I have a record-breaking mind state now. If I didn't, I couldn't have written this book! I want to go above and beyond the same old results. I want to shoot 100%. Crazy? Why? Because someone said so? Who cares what they said? I don't listen to people with limiting beliefs and limited mind states anymore—and starting today I hope you won't either.

*"If you always do what you've always done, you'll always get what you've always got."* —Henry Ford

We need a *new way* because the old way is not evolving us. If we keep putting the same thing in, we are going to keep getting the same thing out. Our best efforts aren't getting us anywhere. Why? Because we don't know what we don't know. We need to aim *way beyond* status quo to surpass it. We need to get back to using our imaginations and dreaming big! Think outside the box? No. Think like there is no box!

The 3 Laws of Shooting Lethality are, in my belief, the *new way*. And don't get me wrong, they are not MY way; they are the way of physics and thus offer the most futuristic and advanced, yet beautifully <u>simple</u> and effortless way to shoot in existence—whether people want to admit it or not. I'm all about real, measurable progress, which is why this handbook also provides many insights and encouragements and includes a lot of wisdom on how to *think* like a leader, innovator, and winner. #NewWayOfThinking. That's what the Lethal Revolution is all about.

For all those reasons and more, if you learn, understand, and devotedly apply the Form, Motion, Mind State, and NeXt Level truths I have shared in the Sniper's Handbook, it is my firm belief that your body and mind will change and your shot will soar to a whole new <u>victorious</u> level, no matter your age (it's never too late!) or skill level.

But it won't just be the wisdom in this book that powers your flight and helps you break your old records; it will be <u>your</u> knowledge, understanding, perseverance, and steadfast devotion to applying it. And that will require humility, openness to change, listening, and patience. Remember this because it is one of the most profound and transformative truths you will ever learn: **Patience is power.**

# LAW 3: The 12 NEXT FACTORS

*"To be wise you must first get wisdom. No matter what it costs, get understanding." Proverbs 4:7*

Congratulations on making it to the third and final LAW of Shooting Lethality: Law #3: NeXt Factors. If you have got a grip on Laws 1 and 2, all you need to do now is incorporate the upgrades in this section and you will be well on your way to becoming a full Level 3 Lethal Sniper. In this section I will be sharing wisdom and insights I have acquired that will help you soar like the eagle you were designed to be and shatter every glass ceiling and record in your sights. #NewWay #RecordBreakingMovement #NWOT

Bear in mind, some of the NeXt Factors are very technical. Don't get intimidated. Work through them slowly. Contact me with your questions and demo requests, and I will get back to you as time allows. With commitment and devotion you'll get it all in time.

As I stated in the last section, with just Laws 1 and 2 you can improve your shot greatly. Technically, if you were to do enough research and analysis, you might be able to figure out the NeXt Factors in this section. By "NeXt Factors" I'm referring to the more advanced aspects of the shot that all work together, such as energy, motion, rhythm, and timing as well as best practices for spirit and soul. Some of the factors will be reinforcements from previous sections, some will be additions. All will be valuable ammo for your shooting machine.

The motion (or "mechanics") of the shot are going to help you better understand *how* the Sniper generates and transfers energy, motion, and perfect timing to shoot so powerfully and effortlessly with such a high degree of accuracy. The energy part alone makes this chapter highly valuable. I will also be discussing the main muscle parts that play the biggest roles through the motion so you know where and how you need to spend your time in the weight room.

The overall goal of mastering energy, motion, and timing is to create a single, undivided, harmonious jump shot with the highest degree of energy and accuracy and the lowest amount of expended energy. Why is low expended energy so important? Because you need every ounce of endurance energy possible to play defense, outplay everyone in the fourth quarter, come from behind, and of course maintain your FORM. I can't say this enough: if your form breaks down in the middle of a game, everything you've worked so hard to master will be lost. Therefore, exerting the least amount of energy when shooting (actually at all times) is of the utmost importance. What all this means: "play smarter not harder."

> **Coach's note:** FORM. I will say this now because I want to make sure it makes it into the book, and I don't want to forget: FORM IS EVERYTHING. That's why we started with it in this book. No matter how well you have mastered the mechanics, if your form breaks down your shot accuracy will decline. Therein lies the absolute necessity of developing both the strength and endurance you need to finish strong with your form still intact.

In this section, I will first share the "ETR" (energy, timing, and rhythm) NeXt Factors, then I will share multiple other factors that will increase your power accuracy, and energy efficiency eXponentially. #NeXtPotentialGains

# NeXt Factor #1: Energy

You can mimic the Blueprint and gain a "breakthrough" mind state, but until you understand the Energy factor (and the other factors), you will be blocked from improving. I stumbled on this game changer while reading an article about the different types of energy. In the article, the author discussed how there are two types of important energy when it comes to motion: Elastic Potential Energy and Kinetic Energy.

- **Elastic Potential Energy** is the <u>possible energy</u> an object (your body!) has based on its stretched or compressed position (think of the crouching Load position in the Blueprint).

- **Kinetic Energy** is the energy that an object (your body!) has based on its motion (think of the "Up" motion energy transfer from your feet to your shooting wrist).

So, when you crouch to jump in the Load position, you load up elastic potential energy. When you jump, it's converted into kinetic energy. What that means is when the ball leaves your hand, it is doing exactly what you instructed it to do based on the kinetic energy motion you transferred to it, which is based on the positional energy potential that produced it.

In other words, the ball's velocity (speed), height, and direction is a direct reflection, a mirror, of your body form (potential energy) and body motion (kinetic energy) during the shot, the same way an arrow's velocity and direction reflect the form and motion of the archer and his bow—which, instructors teach, should be thought of as proverbially *one*. Translation? You + Ball = One. The ball is an extension of you.

For me, that was a game-changing paradigm shift because it made me realize that shooting was simply a positional energy motion that was governed completely by scientific laws, and therefore the more I conformed my form and motion to those laws to create the most simple, direct, and unobstructed energy path from my feet to my wrist, the more often the ball would go in the basket! Talk about *empowering*.

That was the day I knew I had broken through another glass ceiling. That was the day I was liberated from my limiting beliefs and the limiting beliefs of others that had prevented me from believing that I could be a Sniper. I started seeing basketball not through the lens of culture, or coolness, or celebrity, or trophies, but through the lens of science and art and limitless possibility. It was the first day I saw beyond the limits of the past and present to the possibilities of the future. #Breakthrough #NWOT #KnowledgeIsPower #Possibilities

### How Elastic Energy Potential and Kinetic Energy Work

We can look to archery to understand how elastic potential and kinetic energy work in a jump shot. When you pull the arrow back and create tension in the bow and string, the arrow has energy potential; when you let the arrow go, the energy potential is converted into kinetic energy and sends the arrow flying. The velocity (speed) at which the arrow flies depends on how far you pulled the string back (tension), which depends on

95

how strong you are. The accuracy of the arrow depends on your position, form, and stability. The same exact thing applies to shooting hoops.

You need to be in the right form and motion to shoot the ball powerfully and accurately. You begin producing kinetic energy from the time you start the "back and down" groove motion, but full energy potential is not available until you reach the Fire! position. Read that line again. The Fire! position is the position of maximum energy potential. From there, it's simply a matter of extending and shooting in the correct order from bottom to top to ensure it travels a straight, direct, and unobstructed path to your wrist for the final *pop!*

We haven't talk about muscles and muscle groups yet, but for now, just understand they must not only be strong but unified and working together in harmony like a set of cylinders in an engine. There is no room for any division. The closer they work together in harmony and fire in the right order (from bottom to top), the more direct and unopposed kinetic energy will be transferred into the arms and ultimately the ball.

### The Sniper's Power and Accuracy Formula

To be perfectly clear, the velocity and accuracy of your shot are dependent on: 1) your body's position, form, and stability; and 2) how much unopposed upward energy you can generate from your legs and hips. Remember this equation I have developed. I call it the *Sniper's Power and Accuracy Formula*. I believe it is the most important concept to understand for jump shot mastery:

True Foundation + True Form + Unopposed Energy Transfer = Maximum Power and Accuracy.

All this begs the question: now that we know how energy is stored and released through muscles, how can we ensure our muscles work together in HARMONY to produce maximum power? That's where timing comes in.

## NeXt Factor #2: Timing

*"Patience is power. Patience is not an absence of action; rather it is "timing." It waits on the right time to act, for the right principles, and in the right way."*
*— Fulton J. Sheen*

This quote about patience and timing from Fulton Sheen is a universal truth, and it applies to everything in life—jump shots included. If you ask Tiger Woods what the most important part of the golf swing is, I bet *timing* (which, you will see soon, includes body rhythm and harmony) is at the top of his list. Same with great hitters in baseball (especially the homerun bombers).

And same with great shooters and dunkers in basketball. You have to know *when* to pull the trigger.

## Timing Overview

Before we go further, to ensure I haven't lost anyone, so far in this book I have shared the correct <u>form</u> one must take for maximum energy potential and accuracy, the momentum/<u>motion</u> that must be present in order to generate exponential kinetic energy, and now I'm sharing the <u>timing</u> that is needed to transfer as much unopposed kinetic energy at the perfect <u>time</u> for maximum shot power/velocity.

Know and understand this truth: you can be the strongest and most agile basketball shooter in existence, and you can practice more than everyone else, and you can have soaring confidence, but if you lack patience—and we are talking about self-control—to WAIT and ACT (meaning launch to jump and release the ball) at the perfect millisecond, you will hit the dreaded glass ceiling and not be able to move beyond it.

It turns out that the old saying is true: *timing is everything.*

For this reason, it is a scientific fact that you should spend more time developing your shot motion and timing through simple practice in your living room and in front of a mirror to burn the imagery and muscle memory in your mind and body—rather than wasting untold hours at the gym trying to do it on the court. I can assure you when it comes to motion and timing, it's VERY HARD to learn it out on the court. Would be like learning a ballet move out on a stage without the mirror. You need the mirror (and video).

### Timing and Muscle Firing Order

Here's the deal. When you are in the Load position, your muscles are shortened and storing major energy potential to shoot. Alone, they can only generate a certain amount of power to shoot. They need help from the rest of your body and that means you must wait to Fire! until that helps arrives in the form of motion energy from your lower body.

To help understand this, try bending your knees, pausing, then trying to jump straight up. You'll find you can't get jump too high. However, if you bend your knees and swing your arms and torso up without pausing at all (and maybe even add a few steps) to create some motion/momentum, you will find you can jump much higher. Motion generates even more (exponential) kinetic energy and thus jumping and shooting power/velocity.

In order to generate a *lot* of power, the kind of power that propels a high jumper over a bar, or drives a golf ball 300 yards, or fires a basketball high into the air from 20+ feet away, you need much more <u>power</u> than one or two limbs can generate; you need the collective power of <u>all</u> limbs working in perfectly-timed harmony. That means you must release stored energy sequentially from muscle to muscle from the floor to your wrist to create a single bolt of super power to transfer into the ball. That requires that each muscle fires in the right <u>order.</u> #OrderMatters

When you make the "down and back" motion into the Load position, you are doing several things: getting your torso upright, raising the ball to your head, storing up energy potential in your legs *and* generating momentum/motion to generate exponential shooting velocity. Notice I didn't say "<u>jumping</u> velocity." Why? Because you don't need to jump high to make baskets; you just need to efficiently transfer energy from your legs and hips to your arms to fire the ball.

All that said, there are two main things I want to impress here. First, you will need to learn to uncoil each muscle group sequentially from your feet up to your wrist. Second, you cannot hesitate whatsoever at the Load position before you jump. Rather, you must time your launch into the Fire! position wisely to transfer the maximum amount of energy from your feet UP into your arm and wrist in one smooth motion. The key is to roll your hips a little more forward at that critical "up motion" point in the blueprint while beginning to extend your arms to shoot.

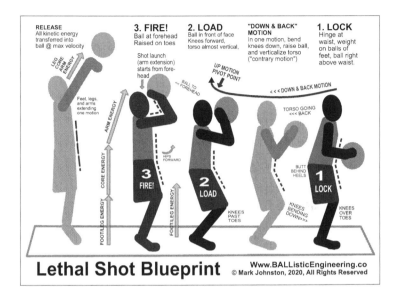

**Lethal Shot Blueprint**

Www.BALListicEngineering.co
© Mark Johnston, 2020, All Rights Reserved

With that in mind, start thinking of the "down and back" motion between the Lock and Load positions not as a transitional <u>motion</u> to get from one form to the other, but as the motion to time the transfer of energy from your lower body to your upper body. As you bend your knees and raise the ball to your head you should be focused on transferring every ounce of motion energy you are generating in your legs to your arms with no energy disruption whatsoever. If you hesitate even the slightest bit in the Load form, you will lose power and accuracy.

You must learn to be patient: first to do the "down and back" move before jumping to shoot, second to shift energy to the "up" motion. Patience is truly power. It will require some work, but you will get it!

### Shot Release Timing

One more thing about timing. Typically, when people discover they don't have enough power to shoot the ball from long range, they hit the weights to get stronger and shoot more. I did the same thing when I kept coming up short. I got strong—especially in my arms and shoulders—with weights. But, despite marginal improvement, I hit a glass ceiling again and couldn't progress any further. It was then I realized that simply getting stronger and shooting more were not going to get me any further.

At that point I was frustrated because I video recorded myself again and it seemed I was doing everything right. I was perplexed. I started to wonder again if maybe having a great jump shot was just a gift that I wasn't given and almost abandoned my commitment to improving. What's weird is that something in my spirit told me there was more to learn, and yet I still doubted it.

> **Coach's note**: *when you feel something in your spirit, don't ignore it. If you hear that inner voice saying things like, "You are so close to the answer, keep seeking and don't give up!" Listen to that voice. It is the voice of Truth!*

## Maximum Kinetic Energy Point

Then one day while showing a guy (who was also a streaky shooter like I used to be) a slow-motion video of a college shooter on my phone—BOOM! The answer I had been seeking was right in front of my eyes. Shockingly, no one had ever pointed this one thing out in all the analysis videos I had watched—at least not in a way I understood it. But there it was, right in front of me now, and the moment I saw it I knew it was gonna be a game changer.

As I watched the slow-motion shooting video, I noticed that the ball left the Sniper's hand a split second before his jump reached its apex. After the ball left his hand, his body continued elevating! I am not a physics master, but I knew precisely what that meant the instant I saw it: it meant I was shooting TOO LATE, after the maximum kinetic energy point (which is right before you have reached the apex of your jump) had passed. #MaxKineticEnergyPoint

That is when I realized I had the form, and I had the energy motion and power, but I didn't have the perfect timing to transfer all my kinetic energy to the ball correctly at the perfect millisecond. In other words, my power was being depleted not because I wasn't strong enough or because I didn't practice enough or because I didn't have the correct form, it was because I wasn't transferring all the power I was generating due to slight hitches in my overall motion. What hitches?

First, I was still slightly hesitating as I transitioned from the Load to the Fire! position. That hesitation was disrupting my momentum and robbing the ball of max kinetic energy and velocity it needed to rise high enough and go far enough to swish. Second, I was not releasing the ball until I was at the top of my jump, which was also robbing the ball of kinetic energy and velocity. Why? Because at the top of your jump all kinetic energy has been depleted! No wonder my arms were overly involved.

## Two Timing Breakthroughs

Finally I came to see why I wasn't improving and it led to two major breakthroughs regarding timing: 1) All the energy my legs and hips were generating separately had to be brought together into one, single harmonious ball of compact energy that blasted into my arms and wrist at the same time so I could pop the ball with maximum velocity without a lot of help from my arms; 2) The only possible way I could bring all the energy from my legs to my arms in one harmonious energy bullet was if I timed their releases perfectly.

In summary, I discovered I had been trying to make the right things happen at the wrong time. Behold, the formula for max compact energy ball velocity: the right amount of energy transferred to the ball at the right time. *Eureka!* Reminder of the Lethal shooting equation:

True Foundation + True Form + Unopposed Energy Transfer = Maximum Power and Accuracy.

> *"I had been trying to make the right things happen at the wrong time." — Mark the Hoopster*

After those game-changing timing discoveries, I was certain I had found the missing link to my shooting woes. When I got to the gym the next morning, I literally ran out to the floor and started shooting. Imagine my shock when I couldn't hit a single basket! Releasing the ball before I reached the top of my extension and jump (and to be clear I mean letting it go on the way up instead of letting it go at the top of my jump or after), felt WEIRD and alien—like the first time I was taught how to swing a golf club the right way after a lifetime of baseball.

So, similar to how Newton discovered the laws of gravity, I started thinking about it all the time, practicing the motion in front of the mirror, recording it, etc.… getting the rhythm and feel for it and focusing on energy transfer from my feet to the ball. Sure enough, my field goal percentage finally started increasing. But then I hit another glass ceiling again.

Why? Because though I was now <u>consciously aware</u> of the hitches in my shooting motion and remedying them, I still hadn't resolved the last chord of the shooting pattern, and that is rhythm. I should note here: becoming consciously aware of the problem was due to my continued knowledge seeking and understanding. Reminder: when you get stuck, and you will, keep seeking knowledge.

## NeXt Factor #3: Rhythm

*"I think the rhythm is the spine of the song. If you change the rhythm, then the song changes as well."* —
*Peter Gabriel*

That is a beautiful and liberating universal truth from Peter Gabriel, one of the greatest songwriters and rhythm masters of all time. If you change just a few words, you'll have some breakthrough wisdom about shooting:

*"I think the rhythm is the spine of the shot. If you change the rhythm, then the shot changes as well."*

### Acquiring Rhythm

Rhythm and timing go hand in hand. I'm a witness: that is 100% true. Rhythm changes everything. Once you have the right form and motion, right mind state, and know the timing essentials, it is a matter of developing a <u>memorable rhythm</u> that brings them all together and harmonizes them in a perfectly-timed, repeatable pattern. And rhythm is something you cannot document; it is something you must *feel.*

So, if I can't document rhythm for you, how can I help you learn it? That is the million-dollar question. Some people say not everyone has rhythm. I say nonsense. I say everyone has been gifted with rhythm, and it's just a matter of developing it (I say the same thing about singing, painting, or any other gift). I am living proof of that.

When I first started making music on a keyboard and drum machine back in 1990, I was so unrhythmical it was comical. But I <u>learned</u> to tap my fingers and feet along with beats from other artists I really liked, and in time I could "keep time" with them. Same thing happened to me as I learned to play the piano "in time." Gradually I could "play the drums" with my hands-on surfaces of all kinds, and then started creating my own rhythms. That's how I learned to rap too.

I was not "born with rhythm." I learned how to be rhythmical through listening, emulating others, practice, and good old <u>perseverance</u>. I stayed committed and the rhythm came. I can now make any kind of beat in any genre of music. And that's how I learned how to add rhythm to my jump shot too. Amazingly, it wasn't until I started watching great shooters' jump shots in full speed motion again that I finally felt the RHYTHM— even heard it like a drum beat in my head—and got a feel for where it ebbed and flowed.

That is when I started thinking of all parts of the shot as one, smooth, "grooving" rhythm like a great drum beat. Now when I coach people I say, "Groove it! Get your rhythm going and in time with the energy transfer from your legs as you rise up."

### Patience and Rhythm

What that discovery, I knew it was finally just a matter of practicing everything I had learned and mastering it: form, motion, breakthrough mindset, timing, and perfect, undivided <u>rhythmical energy transfer</u> ("RET") from my legs to my wrist without any hitches. The challenge for me (and it's still a challenge at times) was that I had to learn to be <u>patient</u> and disciplined though the shot motion and allow the energy (starting in my feet and legs) to unfold and rise upward to my arms and wrist with perfect timing. Why? Because my natural instinct was to quickly gather myself and explode upward and shoot all at once (like many shooters) without creating any rhythm first. #RET

Remember this: when it comes to generating maximum kinetic energy for maximum ball velocity, patience (perfect timing) is power. The more consistent your rhythm and perfect your energy transfer timing from your legs to your arms and wrist, the less unstable arm strength will be required. This is huge. It means even people who aren't buffed and super strong can pop great jumpers from "downtown."

I need to repeat the quote I included at the beginning of this section because it is so amazing and will take you so far in so many ways if you take heed to it:

> "Patience is power. Patience is not an absence of action; rather it is "timing." It waits on the right time to act, for the right principles, and in the right way."
> — Fulton J. Sheen

Meditate on this: patience is power. Patience is all about timing. That truth has profound life implications, but it is also a gold nugget of wisdom about the killer jump shot design. As I alluded to earlier, most people are not patient. We want everything *now* and we are unwilling to delay our gratification. In fact, that's why most people never get ahead financially. I also believe it's one of the main reasons people don't improve their jump shot. That is, they don't want to take the time to learn and even when they do learn, they don't want to take the time to get it right.

If that describes you, don't worry, it describes most people. But you, soaring eagle with a breakthrough mind state, are not most people. You are the rare bird who wants to go to the next level. Therefore, keep in mind the two most important parts of patience:

- Patience 1: to learn and practice the right things right.

- Patience 2: to learn precisely how and where energy is stored and delivered power and accuracy—to the extent that you don't even have to aim anymore.

Bottom line: Develop a rhythmical body motion (or "wave") pattern that you can remember by feel and RELY on in any type of situation. You will eventually need to be able to shoot very fast without thinking about it. It will come. Stay at it and don't break the form. Don't get riled up if you are missing, especially in warm-ups. If you keep missing over and over turn the video recorder on a compare your shot to the Blueprint and recalibrate.

Test your rhythm in different scenarios. Put yourself in "do or die" game situations in practice. Imagine the clock running out. Get the inbounds pass. Hesitate. Bolt to the other side of the court. Hesitate again. Bolt to the elbow. Pump fake. Pull up. Did you hit it? Do it until you can hit it at least 5 times in a row. One of many examples of how to create "game real" situations.

## NeXt Factor #4: Shot Fitness

These are valuable lessons I have learned from my experiences and coaching many others since I first made the devoted commitment to improve my jump shot. What a journey it has been! Pay close attention to these shot upgrades because they are the most common trouble areas that cause shooters to hit glass ceilings. Even now I still break my form and must go back to the Blueprint and recalibrate to get back on track.

### *Foundation*

THIS COMES FIRST! Set your shot house in order on a solid and true foundation, starting with your feet, before you go into the shooting motion. Get your weight balanced perfectly between each leg. 50/50 shared burden! Bar none this is the most common problem I experience in people's shots. Remember: Energy starts at the center of gravity. Get your gravity centered and you'll have concentrated beam of energy to send straight up like a bolt of lightning to your arm. #TakeAStand

111

There are a lot of reasons people don't set their foundation correctly before they shoot but the most common is: they are hurrying. They aren't being patient. This is why I keep telling you "patience is power." You need to be patient in two main ways: 1) to set your foundation; and 2) to groove "back and down" before you jump and extend to shoot. Don't forget this.

I am certain many people will struggle with these two imperative patience points because I have struggled with them as have many shooters I've helped. You will need to retrain your mind and body to be patient repeatedly for a while. Depending on how old you are, you may have to retrain yourself every time you practice or play. People laugh when they hear me talking to myself. I don't care. I am coaching myself: "Mark, be patient. Stop hurrying." Be your own best coach.

---

*Coach's note:* If equal weight on both knees hurts one or both knees, fix them. See a great physical therapist and find out why they are mistracking or hurting and how you can alleviate the pain with rehab and strengthening. Many shooters I encounter favor one leg because of past knee problems. You must overcome knee issues to be a Sniper because the shot requires a double knee bend. I fixed my knee issues with symmetrical strength and flexibility conditioning. Email me if you want a plan.

---

# NeXt Factor #5: Mind Awareness (Higher Consciousness)

Train with conscious awareness of the forms and motions and work through each, but also train in "blind" mode where you don't think about any mechanics and just shoot by feel. Feel of what? Feel of balance and power in your legs, smooth and well-timed rhythmical motion, and kinetic energy passing from legs to arms to wrist to ball at the perfect time.

In games, the only thing you should be consciously aware of is where the ball is, where your defender is, where your teammates are, and setting your foundation correctly before pulling up. If you think about shot mechanics or try to aim, you'll be divided and miss a lot. See "The Shooter's Creed" later in this chapter. Set practice time aside for both mechanics training and blind mode training.

Also, practice with the same state of mind you play. My approach to practice is: there is no practice, only games. Every time on the court is game time. No time to clown around and waste precious time. DO. WORK. The way of the Sniper is focused and high-quality practice time.

There is no such thing as "practice" in the mind of a Sniper. Every single time on the court is do or die game time. I practice like every practice is the last time I will get to play ball. And I make every single shot count as though it were my last. But have fun! Never forget to have fun or you will hit another glass ceiling. Keeping your sense of humor—especially about yourself—is a huge part of having fun.

Oh, one other thing. If you flex you will lose your form. By that I mean if you start trying to show off and impress people, you will lose your form and start missing. Quiet your ego before you step on the court. The great Sniper does not shoot to impress people; he shoots for sport and enjoyment. His eyes and thoughts are fixed on the bullseye, not the spectators. Ignore this wisdom at your own peril.

## NeXt Factor #6: Shot Smoothing

As I alluded to early on, the Lethal shot is technically a two-motion shot (comprised of the "down and back" movement followed by the "up" movement) that you must transform into a one motion shot. If you are like most people, you will probably struggle with this idea initially. Don't get discouraged. Here are some deep insights to help you master smoothing.

The split second you reach the Load position with the ball in front of your face, you should already be starting to jump with your feet and legs *while* bringing your hips the rest of the way forward to verticalize your torso. As you begin to rise, do NOT fire the ball immediately. Instead, as you rise, raise the ball from your face (Load position) to your forehead (the Fire! position), and as soon as it reaches your forehead, THEN fire it.

Why is it so important to raise the ball from your face to your forehead before firing the ball at the rim? Three reasons:

1) The first and most important reason is to give the upward kinetic energy you are generating with your lower body and core time to reach your arms (to feed your arms extra power so your arms are not solely responsible for generating all the ball velocity—which they are incapable of doing in the right trajectory from your face). Patience is power!

2) To start the UP shot motion of your shot with your hips/core and not your arms. Remember, the motion prior to this was "down and back." If you shoot with your arms only from the Load position, you will make a throwing motion rather than an *uplifting* motion and your shot will be flat.

3) To get your torso mostly vertical for maximum straight line direct energy transfer from your core to your arms before firing.

Number 2 might be a tough one to wrap your mind around. I understand. It vexed me for a while too. Let's start with this fact: the shot extension starts in the hips, not the arms. How is that possible? Look at the Blueprint again. Notice the hips and the angled dashed line in the Load position; there is still a bend at the waist and the hips are not fully forward. Now look at the Fire! position. Notice the text "hips forward" with the arrow. Also notice the position of the shooting elbow is well forward.

Let's put it all together now. Here's what has to happen: from the Load position, rise on your toes while extending your legs while rolling your hips forward and as you do, raise the ball from your face to your forehead and FIRE! That short period of time between the time the ball is at your face to the time it gets to your forehead will give your hips time to roll the rest of the way forward to verticalize your torso fully AND send the upward kinetic energy from your legs to your arm!

Also, this is hugely important. Your hand must be UNDER the ball the split second before you fire it. How do you get it in that position on the way up? The key is your upper arm and elbow position. Keep your elbow out front, away from your body, and lift it with your shoulder as you rise, and you'll find your hand automatically goes under the ball. This is something you will need to work out, but it's an absolute necessity for maximum loft, correct trajectory, power, and accuracy. Practice the shooting motion with your hand under the ball and your upper arm parallel with the ground against the side of the backboard.

# NeXt Factor #7: Get Your Arms Out of It

This is also a very common problem with shots. It can be a fatal defect. Most shooters are prone to wanting to shoot with their arms. Resist. Learn to quiet your arms and rather than using them to power the ball to the basket, use them to simply transfer the kinetic energy from your legs and core to the ball.

The more "arm-y" (including the flaring out of your shooting arm) your shot is, the less accurate it will be. The Sniper has a very upward, vertical, simple snap of the arm at the perfect time. Tell your arms you won't be needing their "throwing" services anymore and focus on using them solely to uplift kinetic energy gracefully from your legs and core into the ball.

All that said, there is one thing your right arm must do no matter what, and that is maintain a hard-angled V from the time the ball is in front of your face to the time you fire it. This is actually another patience point you must learn. That tight V is non-negotiable. Why? Because the harder angled the V, the more potential energy you will have to shoot the ball without involving your shoulders.

If you hold that hard-angled V all the way until the ball reaches your forehead, and unleash it at the maximum kinetic energy point, I bet you will start shooting the ball right over the rim (meaning you will be generating much more power). I've seen this happen repeatedly when I am coaching. A person will be shooting air balls or repeatedly hitting the front of the rim and even saying they aren't "strong enough," but then we get their arm coiled and releasing the ball at the perfect time and BOOM! Suddenly they have major power.

THAT kind of uncoiling arm power is GOOD. Why? Because it doesn't require much effort to uncoil. You just shoot at the perfect second and magically your arm has major power without even heaving the ball. Truly magical how kinetic force works. Use it! Oh, and make sure you follow through with a great wrist snap!

## NeXt Factor #8: Shot Training Upgrades

Practice at home: physically and mentally. Practice physically by simply going through the motions fluidly until they are second nature. Practice mentally by visualizing your form and shot for 5 or 10 minutes a day. Science has proven mental visualization is just as effective as physical training. Your mind is powerful. Use it to your advantage. #MindPower

When you first start RE-ENGINEERING your shot (or anything in life), go slow. As my piano teacher once taught me, "Practice at the speed of no mistakes," then gradually speed up and get more intense. Remember, it's one smooth motion: down, back, and up. When you start making a lot of shots, you're gonna be tempted to start bombing a lot of threes. Resist. Master form and motion down before anything else.

Develop the shooting form fundamentals and basic motion from the free-throw line. Master it! You should eventually be able to shoot 90% or better.

Practice your weaknesses, not your strengths. This is so important.

Practice the right things right. Don't take shortcuts. Shortcuts and victory cannot coexist.

Don't worry about swishing. If the ball is going in the basket, you are scoring! This is why I always coach people, "I don't want to see your makes, I want to see your misses." I want to see what happens when the ball is short, or left, or right, or long: do you get a nice bounce and roll, or does it ricochet all over the gym? If the latter, you are going to miss a lot of game time shots no matter how much you swish in practice. If the former, you are going to be unstoppable. "How are your misses going?" This is a new way of thinking (#NWOT), so let it sink in.

Once you get the form and motion down, don't stand around and take set shots in practice. Shoot on the run, off the dribble, stepping back or aside, turning around, taking a pass from both left and right, taking a bad pass, recovering from being off balance, and when absolutely exhausted. After warm-ups and stretching, I do a lot of footwork, sprinting, etc. to get my legs very tired before shooting practice. By the time I start shooting I have the legs of someone who has been playing hard for 30 minutes.

Focus on the front of the rim and visualize the hoop as a cookie jar that you're reaching your hand into with your follow-through. Try to release from your middle finger. If your hand is under the ball and you are almost fully palming it, it will happen by default I find.

After you've started to get command of the shot from mid-range, video record yourself shooting the "33" challenge (how many three-pointers you can make in three minutes getting your own rebounds). You will learn a LOT! Tag me #MarkTheHoopster on IG to let me know your results.

Build your endurance. Google "How to build up my endurance and stamina." Endurance energy is not the same kind of strength as explosive energy.

Remember to let the ball go just before you reach the top of your jump.

Remember, you don't have to start in the Lock position. You can start in the Load position (esp. free throw) or even Fire! position! Just remember, those are serious "neXt level" shooting positions, but you can and will learn them if you work at it. I will be posting instructional videos on shooting from all three positions later.

Always pay attention to what the ball does after it leaves your hands. Remember: the ball is an exact reflection of the energy you transferred into it; nothing more, nothing less. In that sense, the ball is an extension of you. Therein lies the extreme importance of having the correct form, motion, and timing to deliver the most powerful, balanced, and compact JOLT of energy into the ball at the perfect instant to "pop" it out of your arms like a bullet out of a gun.

Play empowering and victorious music when you practice. Get in the victory spirit at all times. Listen to music that supercharges you and helps you BELIEVE in the possibilities. No dark, depressing, mindless stuff or droning podcasts. Get charged. #VictorySpirit

Practice with even more intensity than you play in games. I can't stress the importance of this single upgrade.

# NeXt Factor #9: Strength Upgrades

The body parts that need to be the most flexible for the Lethal shot are hips, hips flexors, abs, lower back, Achilles tendons, calves (especially soleus), quads, and right wrist. The goal is to get these structures elastic, long, and mobile (range of motion in all-natural directions) as possible. Dynamic stretching, heat, and foam roller will help. If you get really knotted up, get trigger-point massage.

For full body stretching, I have developed a full body dynamic stretching routine that I do before practicing/playing and at home on off days. It stretches every single muscle and achieves full range of motion in every joint. I will post it soon after this book is published. It is another game changer. Stay tuned. In the meantime, feel free to YouTube "Full body dynamic stretching routine."

To shoot the Lethal jumper well, you will need great leg strength, especially foot, calves, quads (!), hams, and glutes. You will also need great core strength. It takes some time to develop these muscle groups. Be patient. YouTube is filled with videos on weight training exercises for shooters.

For strengthening, think full body, symmetrical flexibility and strengthening —not just isolated movements like curls, but all sorts of muscular training that challenges your muscles in every possible way. I'm talking slow twitch, fast twitch, plyometrics, stabilization, mobility, whole body fitness (like lifting tires), etc.

One of the guiding light principles I suggest when it comes to muscle resistance is the idea of focusing on strength movements that mimic body demands on the court. Example: I don't stand around and do dumbbell curls. I do them in a half squat position like I am doing a crossover. I even do them on one leg, etc. I also hold 10 or 15 lb. dumbbells and medicine balls and mimic all the forms and motions of the Blueprint in slow motion and fast motion.

Do squats (all kinds), military press, and triceps moves with the same arm alignment as shooting. I also do a combination of different types of movements to challenge my body in every possible way. I will be posting my whole lifting routine soon. Stay tuned! #SymmetricalStrength

It is possible to strengthen with only a few exercises. I did it for two years and it did not adversely impact my shot; in fact, my shot kept improving. They are planks, calf raises on stairs, squats, push-ups, rows, deadlifts, and military press.

Endurance! Train for all kinds of strength, but don't forget ENDURANCE. Hiking, cycling, swimming, running, and other activities will help build your endurance. Don't neglect this all-important strength. If your form breaks down, your game breaks down. I run the mile at least three times a week.

Take care of your back. If your back goes, you're done for a long time. Get super core strong and super core flexible. Learn how to do squats and deadlifts correctly and do not round your back EVER while lifting. Also take care of your knees. If you build major leg, core, and hip strength, and stay flexible, your knees will have to do way less work. I'm 52 and my knees are still incredibly good despite a lifetime of sports and military.

Shoes! So important. You need flexible but supportive shoes. Rigid shoes make the Lethal jump shot hard because it relies so much on foot/Achilles flexibility. Also, I highly recommend orthotics. Here are the ones I use. I added a little foam in the arch, and they are like pro orthotics now. No ankle pain. https://amzn.to/2TkUeea

Overall, you need to be both symmetrically strong and flexible. This will require some work and new habit forming, but it won't take long if you remain committed and devoted. Stay tuned to my IG and YouTube as I will keep sharing more. Also keep a look out for the next book because I'm going to drill deep into every conditioning detail.

# NeXt Factor #10: Body Nutrition

When guys hear that I am age 52 they are generally shocked. The last guy who asked me about my age wanted to know if my "knees were still good." He could not understand how I could be so strong and agile at my age—especially since I had served in the military, ran in boots and 40 lb. ruck sacks, etc. Believe it or not, I don't have good genes or good docs (I can't even afford the deductible!). I just follow wise counsel (God), stay hungry, and take good care of my mind, body, and heart... and that includes eating right.

I recommend sticking to these dietary practices:

- Lean meat (esp. fish and chicken – three times a week)

- Vegan protein from plants

- Whole grains (wheat pasta, brown rice, oats, quinoa, etc.)

- Fruits (prunes, figs, apples, pears, blueberries)

- Veggies (broccoli, Brussel sprouts, sweet potatoes, kale, spinach, etc.)

- Legumes (all kinds, especially beans of all sorts)

125

- Nuts (eat trail mix daily)

- Limit processed sugars to 20 grams per day

- Do intermittent fasting (I prefer the 16:8 – Google it). It benefits both mind and body.

- Avoid toxic food and drink (and people!). I abstain from alcohol and drugs of all sorts because none will make you a better shooter—although they will prevent you from becoming one.

- I Don't do any supplements beside occasional protein shakes. I advise getting all nutrients from food as much as possible.

- Rest. Loads of rest. Try to get 8 or 9 hours a night. Daily 20-30 min. naps are awesome too. Your body is a machine. It needs nutrition and rest to be at its best. This includes meditative prayer time for your soul to strike balance. Balance and moderation are everything.

## NeXt Factor #11: Spiritual Nutrition

To get into a #Breakthrough mind state, your mind may need more than a mind state makeover. You may have a spiritual deficit and might need to do what I did and tear down your whole knowledge house, even the foundation, and rebuild. Don't be afraid to rebuild. Pain is gain. Loss is gain.

If you need a spiritual renewal (many people do), you will need some help. Everyone has their "higher power" preference. Mine is Jesus. I've tried all the other guys, and none even come close. "I can do all things through Christ who strengthens me" (Phil 4:13) is not snake oil. It's a real. I'm proof. This book is proof. Either way, I firmly believe everyone needs a higher power. Here are some mind and spirit transformation tips to get you started:

- Immerse yourself and live by the way of truth always. Mine is the Bible.

- Love yourself. Stop beating yourself up for your failures. God forgives you. Just focus, choose to be happy, and stop doing bad stuff. Things will get better. I truly believe happiness is not a destination but a choice. Choose it daily.

- Wake up. Start being more mentally aware (conscious) of things going on around you. Seek to understand how things and people work. Be curious. "Seek to understand before seeking to be understood" is a principle I live by. Journal your observations. Everything's related.

- Positive affirmations work. Say positive things about yourself. Stop belittling yourself. Read the book "The Tongue is a Creative Force" by Charles Capps and "The Power of Positive Thinking" by Norman Vincent Peale. You won't regret it.

- Visualize success and you will actualize success. You must form a very strong—as in harmonious—mind-body connection to go to the NeXt Level.

- Shut your ego down. Some healthy ego is good for game time, but not a lot. Too much ego will overpower your humility and wreck you. Many players who could have won 10 rings won a lot less or none at all because their egos limited them. You need highly focused, laser-locked concentration and poise to go NeXt Level 3 Sniper.

- Mindfulness helps greatly for practice and games. I've been calling it #CleanSlate. It's when you clear out all your busy thoughts and find some stillness and calm in your mind so you're in the best state to absorb knowledge and understand it... especially ideas that you might have preconceived prejudices against. Open-mindedness is critical for growth.

That said, remember all the law of physics you have built your house on and trust them when you pull up to shoot. I can't emphasize the importance of having faith enough. When I see people not trusting their shot and trying to control the ball with their arms, I encourage them to take "Ten faith shots with total trust they will go in." Every time they start sinking shots. FAITH POWER is real.

- You must master your emotions. It's a process. If you have pent up aggression you need to get rid of it. If you have a girlfriend, or boyfriend, or spouse who is getting you upset, you need to make peace and manage that. Many athletes have hit major glass ceilings because their inability to manage their emotions. The Sniper walks out onto the court with no drama. He is a free man. He walks easy and light and has no crushing heavy burdens on his back (another reason I follow Jesus).

- This is why I believe everyone needs faith in a higher power. I don't care what anyone says. You have to trust something/someone outside of yourself. You alone cannot and should not try to carry the life burden. It will crush you. Take it from me.

- Get over yourself. Your purpose is much bigger than just you. Involve others in your life. Give to others and life will give back to you. Give more than you take. Don't give with expectation. Just give because it's better to give than to receive and truly believe "what comes around goes around." Don't curse yourself. Bless yourself by blessing others. #BeABlessing.

- Pray for humility, faith, discernment, patience, wisdom, and understanding without cease.

- Pursue love. Love of God, love of friend and neighbor, love of family, love of all. Operate with a spirit of gratitude and humility. Be kind and do harm to none yet stand firm in your principles. Don't pay repay evil for evil. Go everywhere as a servant. And "GUARD YOUR HEART above all things for everything you do flows from it." (Proverbs 4:23)

# NeXt Factor #12: Trajectory (and Lethal Sniper's Creed)

I would be remiss if I didn't address life trajectory—as in your purpose and goals of playing hoops. This book might have started with this question, but I wanted to share the form and motion first because I recognize that is why most people bought the book. However, this remains a very important question and the answer WILL influence your ability to elevate to a Level 3 Sniper. The question is:

Why do you play basketball and shoot in the first place? What's your motivation and goal?

If your motivation is winning, you're not alone, but I have come to believe it is not the best motivation for becoming a Lethal Sniper. #NWOT incoming...

Don't get me wrong, winning is a beautiful thing, but it is not everything, and furthermore I personally don't think you should play (let alone live) to win, nor do many of the wisest men who ever walked the earth. I have learned it's best to play out of love and, believe it or not, fun and enjoyment. Yes, I said fun. Sport.

Fun is defined as "light-hearted amusement." I think if you have a #Breakthrough mind state (which is essentially about learning, growth, and continuous improvement), and you are passionate and joyful about what you're doing, the winning will take care of itself. If you are not victorious on the court, you will be victorious off the court. Victory is victory. Keep your mind and heart open to all the forms winning can take. There are many. #Witnessed

Now for a word about motivation from one of the wisest men and most profoundly deep sports psychologists who ever lived. Read and meditate on every line and word. These are words to live by in terms of motivation and competition—life, in fact.

### The Lethal Sniper's Creed

*"When an archer/hoopster is shooting for <u>fun</u> he has all his skill.*

*If he shoots for a brass buckle, he is already nervous. If he shoots for a prize of gold, he goes blind or sees two targets – he is out of his mind.*

*His skill has not changed, but the prize divides him.*

*He thinks more of winning than of shooting.*

*And the need to win <u>drains him of power</u>."*

*-Chuang Tzu (ancient Chinese philosopher)*

To put it as simply as possible, he's saying you will be more powerful and accurate if you shoot for enjoyment and sport rather than for the trophy. Everywhere I look I see this is true. It's no secret that even the most relentless champions in the NBA had deep love for the game and were able to have fun even in the most intense moments. Kobe even made a movie about how much he loved the sport and won an Oscar. Steph is intense but he is always enjoying himself on the court.

If you struggle with this idea, think about other things in your life. I bet you will agree that you've had the most success when you stopped focusing on success and just had fun and enjoyed the journey. I know it holds true for shooting. When I'm shooting for sport and enjoyment, I am totally lights-out. The second I shoot for the trophy and to win, I become divided and my FG percentage starts declining.

All I know is that it's easier to go out and enjoy myself every time without a winning motive. In that way, enjoyment of hoops is a repeatable pattern, and inevitably I make more shots. This speaks to the importance of what I call #Unfocus. It's a totally new way of thinking (#NWOT) so meditate on it and give yourself time to understand it. Sometimes understanding can take a long time. Wait for it. Patience is power.

Sadly, the vast majority of athletes have never heard these words or understood them. That's why, I think, so many reach the pinnacle of sports and find themselves totally unhappy, totally unfulfilled, and totally unwilling to bless others with their gifts. Many think life is all about winning. They haven't learned life is all about love, purpose, passion, and making a positive difference in the world. Winning comes in many forms, but the most important form is love. I truly believe that If you have love, you have it all and everything else is just gravy; although if you don't have love life seems to be empty and have no meaning. That is my experience anyway.

If you're struggling with all this or it rubs you wrong, have no fear. I once struggled with it too. It's a lot to take in. Give it some time to sink in. Here's are a few parting words of encouragement for now.

### Choosing happiness, truth, freedom

The moment you decide to be happy and start focusing on your purpose and passion instead of winning as a means of happiness, you will gradually lose your fear of losing and instead find joy from focusing your energy on *seeking and finding the Truth* that will take you to the next *freedom* level of your purpose and passion.

*"You will know the truth and the truth will make you free." -Jesus*

When you decide to be happy rather than pursue winning as a means of happiness, you decide to be free. You decide to break glass ceilings and records. And magically, that is when true happiness begins. It turns out that the most liberated and happy people in the world are not the ones seeking winning as a means of happiness, but the ones seeking *truth* and the understanding and freedom and joy that blossom from truth. I believe only the ones who are sincerely seeking truth (as opposed to happiness) are both free and happy. And everyone from Jesus to Aristotle agree with me.

Ask yourself this question to figure out where you are: "Who and what do I play for?" Seek to understand the answer to that question and wait for the answer. It might surprise you.

*"Be true to yourself, help others, make each day your masterpiece, make friendship a fine art, drink deeply from good books – especially the Bible, build a shelter against a rainy day, give thanks for your blessings, and pray for guidance every day." – John Wooden, legendary hoops coach*

# Conclusion

*"Don't give up on your dreams,
or your dreams will give up on
you." – John Wooden*

Congratulations for making it to the end of this book. I'm endlessly grateful for your time and willingness to pursue excellence and enjoyment of sport through Lethal shooting knowledge and practice. Everything I've taught you in this book works! Follow these best practices to develop a truly Lethal jump shot.

I have shared everything I know about shot Form, Motion, Mind State, Energy, Timing, Rhythm, and the other NeXt Factors. I have left nothing on court. Armed with that knowledge, understanding, commitment, dedication, and "right things right" smart practice, you will go a long way.

We started with Law #1: Right Form and Motion. We covered the Lethal Shot Blueprint and the Lock, Load, and Fire! forms and motions in it. I explained how the body moves from one form to the next in one, smooth, harmonized motion. We then shifted to Law #2: Right Mind State and discussed the danger of limiting beliefs and how to develop a #Breakthrough mind state to overcome them. We then went on to Law #3: The 12 NeXt Factors, which covered how energy, timing, and rhythm work together to create maximum power and accuracy.

As I said in the beginning, from here it's all on you... your commitment, your devotion, your journaling, your progress tracking, your obedience to the laws of physics and meta-physics, your motive power, your mind state, your spirit, and your love and passion. Yes, your love.

I would be totally remiss if I didn't round this learning journey out with the greatest lesson that I have ever learned. It's the lesson I learned that formed my "new way" foundation when I decided to tear it all down and rebuild from the ground up. It is this:

> *"I can have everything under the sun, but if I don't have love, I have nothing." — St. Paul*

That is the truth that ultimately set me free and changed my heart and mind about everything. It is the truth that brought me fulfillment and peace of mind that allowed me to finally get over myself, live in the present and hope in the future, and be grateful for all the gifts of talent, friendship, and love the Lord has given me. It is the truth I rebuilt my life, my marriage, my career, and my hoops game on, and I've been building and growing more and more every day since. If you want my full formula for success in whatever you do, it is this:

Truth (knowledge) = Freedom. What kind of freedom? Freedom to love and be loved, enjoy life, thrive in life, find your purpose and passion, and make a positive difference in the world through the sharing of your gifts with others—especially basketball because it brings people together and we need togetherness now more than ever! The BALListic Revolution isn't just about great shooting; it's about great thinking and great living too.

God speed and hoops excellence! Now go, soar like an eagle and be victorious. And don't forget to tell me about your progress on IG with hashtag #MarkTheHoopster. Thank you and God bless you!

Shoot for the moon. #Moonshot

Much love in truth,

Mark the Hoopster (formerly known as Frank Gamble)

PS: If you've been wondering who the great "Sniper" is, the great Sniper is <u>you</u>.

PPS: There are no glass ceilings. They are illusions. Your only real foe is you. Though it cost you everything you have, get knowledge and understanding!

> *Wherever you go, go with all your heart."* — *Confucius* "

# A Few More Things

## Please Share Your Testimonies

We want to hear about your progress. Post your vids and testimonials on YouTube and IG. Hashtag me #MarkTheHoopster and let me know! I am mark_the_hoopster on IG.

## Sniper Training

We do in-person and on-site individual and group Sniper training for any age or size group. Please contact us at hoopsterclubofficial@gmail.com with your requirements and we will send you a custom quote.

## Sniper Trainer Certification

Interesting in becoming a certified Sniper Trainer? Contact us at info@hoopsters.club and send us a video of you hitting ten shots in a row from all over the floor using the Killer jump shot form with a 2 minute video explaining why you would make a great trainer, and we will get back to you. Thanks!

## Charity Support

We support multiple charities and a portion of proceeds from the book will be sent to them.

# Training Video

Please see our web page <u>www.hoopsters.club</u> or YouTube channel (Mark the Hoopster) for training videos. We are working on them now.

## Training Video Insights

Here's what you need to understand when it comes to "ETR" NeXt Factors and the Lethal Shot. The Lethal Shot is a WHOLE BODY shot. As you hopefully saw in the video, I explained how kinetic energy is gathered through the whole body and transferred up to the wrist with perfect timing. That is, you don't shoot primarily with your legs or arms or wrists; you shoot with your whole body. Your arms are not the primary means of shooting; your arms are more like sling shots that transfer the lower-body kinetic energy into the ball.

In order to shoot the most powerful, accurate, and energy-efficient shot possible, your mind must orchestrate every muscle to work in perfect sync. and rhythm from the second you bend your knees through the final snap of the wrist. Now you can see why it is so incredibly important for your mind and body to be undivided. The Lethal Shot is pure HARMONY of all body parts working together as one (like a symphony of different instruments) to create maximum energy potential from the floor to the fingertip of his middle finger to release the ball upward with maximum ballistic velocity. For this reason alone you will do well to keep all intoxicants out of your shooting machine—especially mind-altering ones. #BALListicShooting

# Breakthrough Affirmations

"I believe I have unlimited potential and I will be victorious."

"I believe knowledge, commitment, devotion, perseverance, and practicing the right things right are the keys to victory."

"I believe the quality of practice is way more important than the quantity of practice."

"I believe in the laws of physics, and I believe they totally override anyone's personal opinion about shooting or basketball."

"I believe I can shoot 100% from the floor against anyone if my form, motion, mind, and body are right and harmonious."

"I believe the only thing that can prevent me from continuously improving is my own lack of knowledge and failure to remain committed and devoted."

"I believe anything is possible. Just because I can't see or comprehend something right now doesn't mean it's impossible."

"I believe I am a blessed, gifted person with unlimited potential who can never fail. There are no fails or setbacks, only learning and continuous improvement."

"I believe fear is the result of ignorance. Therefore, when I fear something, I will seek knowledge to understand what I am lacking so I can overcome it."

"I believe my mind and body must be harmonious, healthy, and undivided. Therefore, I will seek understanding and peace at all times."

"I believe with all my heart and mind and spirit that I will be a Lethal shooter and break all kinds of records."

"I believe in paying it forward, so I will always focus not on winning and being better than others, but on learning and growing so I can help others learn and grow."

#NWOT #BREAKTHROUGH

# Lethal Blueprint

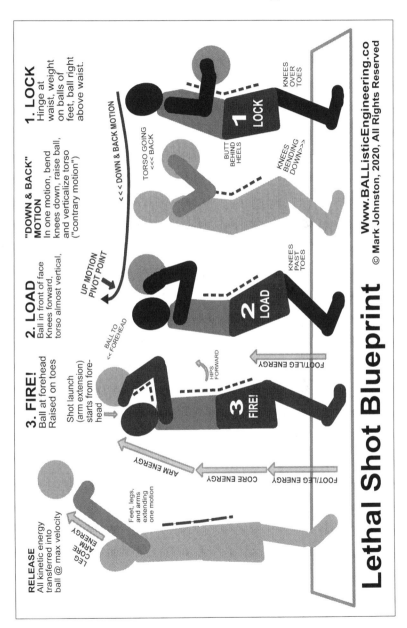

**1. LOCK**
Hinge at waist, weight on balls of feet, ball right above waist.

**"DOWN & BACK" MOTION**
In one motion, bend knees down, raise ball, and verticalize torso ("contrary motion")

<<< DOWN & BACK MOTION

**2. LOAD**
Ball in front of face Knees forward, torso almost vertical,

UP MOTION PIVOT POINT

BALL TO FOREHEAD

**3. FIRE!**
Ball at forehead Raised on toes

Shot launch (arm extension) starts from forehead

HIPS FORWARD

FOOT/LEG ENERGY

**RELEASE**
All kinetic energy transferred into ball @ max velocity

Feet, legs, and arms extending one motion

LEG CORE ARM ENERGY

ARM ENERGY

CORE ENERGY

FOOT/LEG ENERGY

LOCK
BUTT BEHIND HEELS
TORSO GOING <<< BACK
KNEES BENDING DOWN>>>
KNEES OVER TOES

LOAD
KNEES PAST TOES

FIRE!

## Lethal Shot Blueprint

First 20 people who see this message and email us at <u>hoopstersclubofficial@gmail.com</u> will get a free NWOT sticker + shipping. ☺

Made in the USA
San Bernardino, CA
27 March 2020